History & Geography 1200
Teacher's Guide

W9-CBB-644

CONTENTS

Author: Alpha Omega Publications
Editor: Alan Christopherson, M.S.

Alpha Omega Publications®

804 N. 2nd Ave. E., Rock Rapids, IA 51246-1759
© MM by Alpha Omega Publications, Inc.   All rights reserved.
LIFEPAC is a registered trademark of Alpha Omega Publications, Inc.

OVERVIEW

HISTORY & GEOGRAPHY

Curriculum Overview
Grades 1–12

	Grade 1	Grade 2	Grade 3
LIFEPAC 1	**I AM A SPECIAL PERSON** • God made me • You are God's child • All about you • Using proper manners	**FAMILIES AND NEIGHBORS** • We need a family • We help our family • Our neighborhood • Helping our neighbors	**FISHING IN MAINE** • At look at Deer Island • A lobster boat • Planting lobster traps • Catching lobsters
LIFEPAC 2	**COMMUNICATING WITH SOUND** • Sounds people make • Sounds that communicate • Communicating without sound • Communicating with God	**COMMUNITY HELPERS** • What is a community • Community helpers • Your church community • Helping your community	**FARMING IN KANSAS** • The six parts of Kansas • Getting to know Kansas • Exploring Kansas • Harvest in Kansas
LIFEPAC 3	**I HAVE FEELINGS** • I feel sad • I feel afraid • I feel happy • I have other feelings	**NEIGHBORHOOD STORES** • Pioneer goods and services • Modern goods and services • Some business rules • God's business rules	**FRUIT-GROWING IN WASHINGTON** • Geography of Washington • Cities in Washington • Apple blossom time • Apple harvest time
LIFEPAC 4	**I LIVE IN A FAMILY** • My mother and father • My brothers and sisters • My grandparents • What my family does	**FARMS AND CITIES** • Farming long ago • Farming today • Growing cities • Changing cities	**FORESTS IN OREGON** • A land of forests • Trees of the forests • Lumbering in Oregon • Keeping Oregon's forests
LIFEPAC 5	**YOU AND GOD'S FAMILY** • Getting ready in the morning • Walking to school • The school family • The church family	**NEIGHBORS AROUND THE WORLD** • Things all families need • How communities share • How communities change • Customs of the world	**CALIFORNIA: A GOLDEN LAND** • Early California • The ranch community • A trip around the state • Work on a truck farm
LIFEPAC 6	**PLACES PEOPLE LIVE** • Life on the farm • Life in the city • Life by the sea	**A JAPANESE FAMILY** • Places people live in Japan • School in Japan • Work in Japan • Play in Japan	**CATTLE IN TEXAS** • Learning about Texas • Early ranches in Texas • Life on a ranch • A cattle round-up
LIFEPAC 7	**COMMUNITY HELPERS** • Firemen and policemen • Doctors • City workers • Teachers and ministers	**HOW WE TRAVEL** • Travel in Bible times • Travel in the past • Travel today • Changes in today's world	**COAL MINING IN PENNSYLVANIA** • The formation of coal • Products from coal • Methods of mining coal • The state of Pennsylvania
LIFEPAC 8	**I LOVE MY COUNTRY** • America discovered • The Pilgrims • The United States begin • Respect for your country	**MESSAGES FROM FAR AND NEAR** • Communication in Bible times • Communication today • Reasons for communication • Communication without sound	**MANUFACTURING IN MICHIGAN** • Facts about Michigan • Interesting people of Michigan • Places in Michigan • The treasures in Michigan
LIFEPAC 9	**I LIVE IN THE WORLD** • The globe • Countries • Friends in Mexico • Friends in Japan	**CARING FOR OUR NEIGHBORHOODS** • God's plan for nature • Sin changed nature • Problems in our neighborhoods • Helping our neighborhoods	**SPACE TRAVEL IN FLORIDA** • A place to launch spacecraft • Worker at the Space Center • The first flights • The trip to the moon
LIFEPAC 10	**THE WORLD AND YOU** • You are special • Your family • Your school and church • Your world	**PEOPLE DEPEND ON EACH OTHER** • Depending on our families • Depending on our neighbors • Depending on our communities • Communicating with God	**REVIEW OF NINE STATES** • California and Kansas • Washington and Maine • Oregon and Pennsylvania • Texas, Florida, and Michigan

Grade 4	Grade 5	Grade 6	
OUR EARTH • The surface of the earth • Early explorations of the earth • Exploring from space • Exploring the oceans	**A NEW WORLD** • Exploration of America • The first colonies • Conflict with Britain • Birth of the United States	**WORLD GEOGRAPHY** • Latitude and longitude • Western and eastern hemispheres • The southern hemisphere • Political and cultural regions	LIFEPAC 1
SEAPORT CITIES • Sydney • Hong Kong • Istanbul • London	**A NEW NATION** • War for Independence • Life in America • A new form of government • The Nation's early years	**THE CRADLE OF CIVILIZATION** • Mesopotamia • The land of Israel • The Nation of Israel • Egypt	LIFEPAC 2
DESERT LANDS • What is a desert? • Where are the deserts? • How do people live in the desert?	**A TIME OF TESTING** • Louisiana Purchase • War of 1812 • Sectionalism • Improvements in trade & travel	**GREECE AND ROME** • Geography of the region • Beginning civilizations • Contributions to other civilizations • The influence of Christianity	LIFEPAC 3
GRASSLANDS • Grasslands of the world • Ukraine • Kenya • Argentina	**A GROWING NATION** • Andrew Jackson's influence • Texas & Oregon • Mexican War • The Nation divides	**THE MIDDLE AGES** • The feudal system • Books and schools • The Crusades • Trade and architecture	LIFEPAC 4
TROPICAL RAIN FORESTS • Facts about rain forests • Rain forests of the world • The Amazon rain forest • The Congo rain forest	**A DIVIDED NATION** • Civil War • Reconstruction • Gilded Age • The need for reform	**SIX SOUTH AMERICAN COUNTRIES** • Brazil • Colombia • Venezuela • Three Guianas	LIFEPAC 5
THE POLAR REGIONS • The polar regions: coldest places in the world • The Arctic polar region • The Antarctic polar region	**A CHANGING NATION** • Progressive reforms • Spanish-American War • World War I • Roaring Twenties	**OTHER AMERICAN COUNTRIES** • Ecuador and Peru • Bolivia and Uruguay • Paraguay and Argentina • Chile	LIFEPAC 6
MOUNTAIN COUNTRIES • Peru – the Andes • The Incas and modern Peru • Nepal – the Himalayas • Switzerland – the Alps	**DEPRESSION AND WAR** • The Great Depression • War begins in Europe • War in Europe • War in the Pacific	**AFRICA** • Geography and cultures • Countries of northern Africa • Countries of central Africa • Countries of southern Africa	LIFEPAC 7
ISLAND COUNTRIES • Islands of the earth • Cuba • Iceland • Japan	**COLD WAR** • Korean War & other crises • Vietnam War • Civil Rights Movement • Upheaval in America	**MODERN WESTERN EUROPE** • The Renaissance • The Industrial Revolution • World War I • World War II	LIFEPAC 8
NORTH AMERICA • Geography • Lands, lakes and rivers • Northern countries • Southern countries	**INTO THE NEW MILLENNIUM** • Watergate and détente • The fall of Communism • The Persian Gulf • Issues of the new millennium	**MODERN EASTERN EUROPE** • Early government • Early churches • Early countries • Modern countries	LIFEPAC 9
OUR WORLD IN REVIEW • Europe and the explorers • Asia and Africa • Southern continents • North America, North Pole	**THE UNITED STATES OF AMERICA** • Beginning America until 1830 • Stronger America 1830-1930 • 1930 to the end of the millennium • The new millennium	**THE DEVELOPMENT OF OUR WORLD** • Cradle of civilization • The Middle Ages • Modern Europe • South America and Africa	LIFEPAC 10

	Grade 7	Grade 8	Grade 9
LIFEPAC 1	**WHAT IS HISTORY** • Definition and significance of history • Historians and the historical method • Views of history	**EUROPE COMES TO AMERICA** • Voyages of Columbus • Spanish exploration • Other exploration • The first colonies	**UNITED STATES HERITAGE** • American colonies • Acquisitions and annexations • Backgrounds to freedom • Backgrounds to society
LIFEPAC 2	**WHAT IS GEOGRAPHY** • Classes of geography • Geography and relief of the earth • Maps and the study of our world • Time zones	**BRITISH AMERICA** • English colonies • Government • Lifestyle • Wars with France	**OUR NATIONAL GOVERNMENT** • Ideals of national government • National government developed • Legislative and Executive branches • Judicial branch
LIFEPAC 3	**U.S. HISTORY AND GEOGRAPHY** • Geography of the U.S. • Early history of the U.S. • Physical regions of the U.S. • Cultural regions of the U.S.	**THE AMERICAN REVOLUTION** • British control • Rebellion of the Colonies • War for independence • Constitution	**STATE AND LOCAL GOVERNMENT** • Powers of state government • County government • Township government • City government
LIFEPAC 4	**ANTHROPOLOGY** • Understanding anthropology • The unity of man • The diversity of man • The culture of man	**A FIRM FOUNDATION** • Washington's presidency • Adams administration • Jeffersonian Democracy • War of 1812	**PLANNING A CAREER** • Definition of a career • God's will concerning a career • Selecting a career • Preparation for a career
LIFEPAC 5	**SOCIOLOGY** • Sociology defined • Historical development • Importance to Christians • Method of sociology	**A GROWING NATION** • Jacksonian Era • Northern border • Southern border • Industrial Revolution	**CITIZENSHIP** • Citizenship defined • Gaining citizenship • Rights of citizenship • Responsibilities of citizenship
LIFEPAC 6	**U.S. ANTHROPOLOGY** • Cultural background of the U.S. • Native American cultures • Cultures from distant lands • Cultural and social interaction	**THE CIVIL WAR** • Division & Secession • Civil War • Death of Lincoln • Reconstruction	**THE EARTH AND MAN** • Man inhabits the earth • Man's home on the earth • Man develops the earth • The future of the earth
LIFEPAC 7	**ECONOMICS** • Economics defined • Methods of the economist • Tools of the economist • An experiment in economy	**GILDED AGE TO PROGRESSIVE ERA** • Rise of industry • Wild West • America as a world power • Progressive era	**REGIONS OF THE WORLD** • A region defined • Geographic and climate regions • Cultural and political regions • Economic regions of Europe
LIFEPAC 8	**POLITICAL SCIENCE** • Definition of political science • Roots of Western thought • Modern political thinkers • Political theory	**A WORLD IN CONFLICT** • World War I • Great Depression • New Deal • World War II	**MAN AND HIS ENVIRONMENT** • The physical environment • Drug abuse • The social environment • Man's responsibilities
LIFEPAC 9	**STATE ECONOMICS AND POLITICS** • Background of state government • State government • State finance • State politics	**COLD WAR AMERICA** • Origins of the Cold War • Vietnam • Truman to Nixon • Ending of the Cold War	**TOOLS OF THE GEOGRAPHER** • The globe • Types of maps • Reading maps • The earth in symbol form
LIFEPAC 10	**SOCIAL SCIENCES REVIEW** • History and geography • Anthropology • Sociology • Economics and politics	**RECENT AMERICA & REVIEW** • Europe to independence • Colonies to the Civil War • Civil War to World War II • World War II through Cold War	**MAN IN A CHANGING WORLD** • Development of the nation • Development of government • Development of the earth • Solving problems

Grade 10	Grade 11	Grade 12	
ANCIENT CIVILIZATION • Origin of civilization • Early Egypt • Assyria and Babylonia • Persian civilization	**FOUNDATIONS OF DEMOCRACY** • Democracy develops • Virginia • New England colonies • Middle and southern colonies	**INTERNATIONAL GOVERNMENTS** • Why have governments • Types of governments • Governments in our world • Political thinkers	LIFEPAC 1
ANCIENT CIVILIZATIONS • India • China • Greek civilization • Roman Empire	**CONSTITUTIONAL GOVERNMENT** • Relations with England • The Revolutionary War • Articles of Confederation • Constitution of the U.S.	**UNITED STATES GOVERNMENT** • U.S. Constitution • Bill of Rights • Three branches of government • Legislative process	LIFEPAC 2
THE MEDIEVAL WORLD • Introduction to the Middle Ages • Early Middle Ages • Middle Ages in transition • High Middle Ages	**NATIONAL EXPANSION** • A strong federal government • Revolution of 1800 • War of 1812 • Nationalism and sectionalism	**AMERICAN PARTY SYSTEM** • American party system • Development political parties • Functions of political parties • Voting	LIFEPAC 3
RENAISSANCE AND REFORMATION • Changes in government and art • Changes in literature and thought • Advances in science • Reform within the Church	**A NATION DIVIDED** • Issues of division • Division of land and people • Economics of slavery • Politics of slavery	**HISTORY OF GOVERNMENTS** • Primitive governments • Beginnings of Democracy • Feudalism, Theocracy & Democracy • Fascism & Nazism	LIFEPAC 4
GROWTH OF WORLD EMPIRES • England and France • Portugal and Spain • Austria and Germany • Italy and the Ottoman Empire	**A NATION UNITED AGAIN** • Regionalism • The division • The Civil War • Reconstruction	**THE CHRISTIAN & GOVERNMENT** • Discrimination & the Christian • Christian attitudes • "Opinion & Truth" in politics • Politics & Propaganda	LIFEPAC 5
THE AGE OF REVOLUTION • Factors leading to revolution • The English Revolution • The American Revolution • The French Revolution	**INVOLVEMENT AT HOME & ABROAD** • Surge of industry • The industrial lifestyle • Isolationism • Involvement in conflict	**FREE ENTERPRISE** • Economics • Competition • Money through history • International finance & currency	LIFEPAC 6
THE INDUSTRIAL REVOLUTION • Sparks of preparation • Industrial revolution in England • Industrial revolution in America • Social changes of the revolution	**THE SEARCH FOR PEACE** • The War and its aftermath • The Golden Twenties • The Great Depression • The New Deal	**BUSINESS AND YOU** • Running a business • Government & business • Banks & Mergers • Deregulation & Bankruptcy	LIFEPAC 7
TWO WORLD WARS • Mounting tension • World War I • Peace and power quests • World War II	**A NATION AT WAR** • Causes of the war • World War II • Korean Conflict • Vietnam Conflict	**THE STOCK MARKET** • How it started and works • Selecting stocks • Types of stocks • Tracking stocks	LIFEPAC 8
THE CONTEMPORARY WORLD • The Cold War • Korean War and Vietnam War • Collapse of the Soviet Union • Today's world	**CONTEMPORARY AMERICA** • America in the 1960s • America in the 1970s • America in the 1980s & 90s • International Scene 1980–Present	**BUDGET AND FINANCE** • Cash, Credit & Checking • Buying a car • Grants, Loans & IRAs • Savings & E-cash	LIFEPAC 9
ANCIENT TIMES TO THE PRESENT • Ancient civilizations • Medieval times • The Renaissance • The modern world	**UNITED STATES HISTORY** • Basis of democracy • The 1800s • Industrialization • Current history	**GEOGRAPHY AND REVIEW** • Euro & International finance • U.S. Geography • The global traveler • Neighbors, Heroes & The Holy Land	LIFEPAC 10

MANAGEMENT

STRUCTURE OF THE LIFEPAC CURRICULUM

The LIFEPAC curriculum is conveniently structured to provide one teacher handbook containing teacher support material with answer keys and ten student worktexts for each subject at grade levels two through twelve. The worktext format of the LIFEPACs allows the student to read the textual information and complete workbook activities all in the same booklet. The easy to follow LIFEPAC numbering system lists the grade as the first number(s) and the last two digits as the number of the series. For example, the Language Arts LIFEPAC at the 6th grade level, 5th book in the series would be LAN0605.

Each LIFEPAC is divided into 3 to 5 sections and begins with an introduction or overview of the booklet as well as a series of specific learning objectives to give a purpose to the study of the LIFEPAC. The introduction and objectives are followed by a vocabulary section which may be found at the beginning of each section at the lower levels, at the beginning of the LIFEPAC in the middle grades, or in the glossary at the high school level. Vocabulary words are used to develop word recognition and should not be confused with the spelling words introduced later in the LIFEPAC. The student should learn all vocabulary words before working the LIFEPAC sections to improve comprehension, retention, and reading skills.

Each activity or written assignment has a number for easy identification, such as 1.1. The first number corresponds to the LIFEPAC section and the number to the right of the decimal is the number of the activity.

Teacher checkpoints, which are essential to maintain quality learning, are found at various locations throughout the LIFEPAC. The teacher should check 1) neatness of work and penmanship, 2) quality of understanding (tested with a short oral quiz), 3) thoroughness of answers (complete sentences and paragraphs, correct spelling, etc.), 4) completion of activities (no blank spaces), and 5) accuracy of answers as compared to the answer key (all answers correct).

The self test questions are also number coded for easy reference. For example, 2.015 means that this is the 15th question in the self test of Section II. The first number corresponds to the LIFEPAC section, the zero indicates that it is a self test question, and the number to the right of the zero the question number.

The LIFEPAC test is packaged at the centerfold of each LIFEPAC. It should be removed and put aside before giving the booklet to the student for study.

Answer and test keys have the same numbering system as the LIFEPACs and appear at the back of this handbook. The student may be given access to the answer keys (not the test keys) under teacher supervision so that he can score his own work.

A thorough study of the Curriculum Overview by the teacher before instruction begins is essential to the success of the student. The teacher should become familiar with expected skill mastery and understand how these grade level skills fit into the overall skill development of the curriculum. The teacher should also preview the objectives that appear at the beginning of each LIFEPAC for additional preparation and planning.

TEST SCORING and GRADING

Answer keys and test keys give examples of correct answers. They convey the idea, but the student may use many ways to express a correct answer. The teacher should check for the essence of the answer, not for the exact wording. Many questions are high level and require thinking and creativity on the part of the student. Each answer should be scored based on whether or not the main idea written by the student matches the model example. "Any Order" or "Either Order" in a key indicates that no particular order is necessary to be correct.

Most self tests and LIFEPAC tests at the lower elementary levels are scored at 1 point per answer; however, the upper levels may have a point system awarding 2 to 5 points for various answers or questions. Further, the total test points will vary; they may not always equal 100 points. They may be 78, 85, 100, 105, etc.

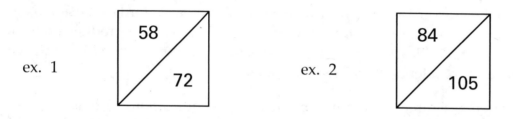

A score box similar to ex.1 above is located at the end of each self test and on the front of the LIFEPAC test. The bottom score, 72, represents the total number of points possible on the test. The upper score, 58, represents the number of points your student will need to receive an 80% or passing grade. If you wish to establish the exact percentage that your student has achieved, find the total points of his correct answers and divide it by the bottom number (in this case 72.) For example, if your student has a point total of 65, divide 65 by 72 for a grade of 90%. Referring to ex. 2, on a test with a total of 105 possible points, the student would have to receive a minimum of 84 correct points for an 80% or passing grade. If your student has received 93 points, simply divide the 93 by 105 for a percentage grade of 89%. Students who receive a score below 80% should review the LIFEPAC and retest using the appropriate Alternate Test found in the Teacher's Guide.

The following is a guideline to assign letter grades for completed LIFEPACs based on a maximum total score of 100 points.

LIFEPAC Test	=	60% of the Total Score (or percent grade)
Self Test	=	25% of the Total Score (average percent of self tests)
Reports	=	10% or 10* points per LIFEPAC
Oral Work	=	5% or 5* points per LIFEPAC

*Determined by the teacher's subjective evaluation of the student's daily work.

Example:

LIFEPAC Test Score	=	92%	92	x .60	=	55 points
Self Test Average	=	90%	90	x .25	=	23 points
Reports					=	8 points
Oral Work					=	4 points

TOTAL POINTS = 90 points

Grade Scale based on point system:

100	–	94	=	A
93	–	86	=	B
85	–	77	=	C
76	–	70	=	D
Below		70	=	F

TEACHER HINTS and STUDYING TECHNIQUES

LIFEPAC Activities are written to check the level of understanding of the preceding text. The student may look back to the text as necessary to complete these activities; however, a student should never attempt to do the activities without reading (studying) the text first. Self tests and LIFEPAC tests are never open book tests.

Language arts activities (skill integration) often appear within other subject curriculum. The purpose is to give the student an opportunity to test his skill mastery outside of the context in which it was presented.

Writing complete answers (paragraphs) to some questions is an integral part of the LIFEPAC Curriculum in all subjects. This builds communication and organization skills, increases understanding and retention of ideas, and helps enforce good penmanship. Complete sentences should be encouraged for this type of activity. Obviously, single words or phrases do not meet the intent of the activity, since multiple lines are given for the response.

Review is essential to student success. Time invested in review where review is suggested will be time saved in correcting errors later. Self tests, unlike the section activities, are closed book. This procedure helps to identify weaknesses before they become too great to overcome. Certain objectives from self tests are cumulative and test previous sections; therefore, good preparation for a self test must include all material studied up to that testing point.

The following procedure checklist has been found to be successful in developing good study habits in the LIFEPAC curriculum.

1. Read the introduction and Table of Contents.
2. Read the objectives.
3. Recite and study the entire vocabulary (glossary) list.
4. Study each section as follows:
    a. Read the introduction and study the section objectives.
    b. Read all the text for the entire section, but answer none of the activities.
    c. Return to the beginning of the section and memorize each vocabulary word and definition.
    d. Reread the section, complete the activities, check the answers with the answer key, correct all errors, and have the teacher check.
    e. Read the self test but do not answer the questions.
    f. Go to the beginning of the first section and reread the text and answers to the activities up to the self test you have not yet done.
    g. Answer the questions to the self test without looking back.
    h. Have the self test checked by the teacher.
    i. Correct the self test and have the teacher check the corrections.
    j. Repeat steps a–i for each section.

5. Use the SQ3R method to prepare for the LIFEPAC test.
   Scan the whole LIFEPAC.
   Question yourself on the objectives.
   Read the whole LIFEPAC again.
   Recite through an oral examination.
   Review weak areas.
6. Take the LIFEPAC test as a closed book test.
7. LIFEPAC tests are administered and scored under direct teacher supervision. Students who receive scores below 80% should review the LIFEPAC using the SQ3R study method and take the Alternate Test located in the Teacher Handbook. The final test grade may be the grade on the Alternate Test or an average of the grades from the original LIFEPAC test and the Alternate Test.

GOAL SETTING and SCHEDULES

Each school must develop its own schedule, because no single set of procedures will fit every situation. The following is an example of a daily schedule that includes the five LIFEPAC subjects as well as time slotted for special activities.

Possible Daily Schedule

8:15	–	8:25	Pledges, prayer, songs, devotions, etc.
8:25	–	9:10	Bible
9:10	–	9:55	Language Arts
9:55	–	10:15	Recess (juice break)
10:15	–	11:00	Math
11:00	–	11:45	History & Geography
11:45	–	12:30	Lunch, recess, quiet time
12:30	–	1:15	Science
1:15	–		Drill, remedial work, enrichment*

*Enrichment: Computer time, physical education, field trips, fun reading, games and puzzles, family business, hobbies, resource persons, guests, crafts, creative work, electives, music appreciation, projects.

Basically, two factors need to be considered when assigning work to a student in the LIFEPAC curriculum.

The first is time. An average of 45 minutes should be devoted to each subject, each day. Remember, this is only an average. Because of extenuating circumstances a student may spend only 15 minutes on a subject one day and the next day spend 90 minutes on the same subject.

The second factor is the number of pages to be worked in each subject. A single LIFEPAC is designed to take 3 to 4 weeks to complete. Allowing about 3-4 days for LIFEPAC introduction, review, and tests, the student has approximately 15 days to complete the LIFEPAC pages. Simply take the number of pages in the LIFEPAC, divide it by 15 and you will have the number of pages that must be completed on a daily basis to keep the student on schedule. For example, a LIFEPAC containing 45 pages will require 3 completed pages per day. Again, this is only an average. While working a 45 page LIFEPAC, the student may complete only 1 page the first day if the text has a lot of activities or reports, but go on to complete 5 pages the next day.

Long range planning requires some organization. Because the traditional school year originates in the early fall of one year and continues to late spring of the following year, a calendar should be devised that covers this period of time. Approximate beginning and completion dates can be noted on the calendar as well as special occasions such as holidays, vacations and birthdays. Since each LIFEPAC takes 3-4 weeks or eighteen days to complete, it should take about 180 school days to finish a set of ten LIFEPACs. Starting at the beginning school date, mark off eighteen school days on the calendar and that will become the targeted completion date for the first LIFEPAC. Continue marking the calendar until you have established dates for the remaining nine LIFEPACs making adjustments for previously noted holidays and vacations. If all five subjects are being used, the ten established target dates should be the same for the LIFEPACs in each subject.

FORMS

The sample weekly lesson plan and student grading sheet forms are included in this section as teacher support materials and may be duplicated at the convenience of the teacher.

The student grading sheet is provided for those who desire to follow the suggested guidelines for assignment of letter grades found on page 3 of this section. The student's self test scores should be posted as percentage grades. When the LIFEPAC is completed the teacher should average the self test grades, multiply the average by .25 and post the points in the box marked self test points. The LIFEPAC percentage grade should be multiplied by .60 and posted. Next, the teacher should award and post points for written reports and oral work. A report may be any type of written work assigned to the student whether it is a LIFEPAC or additional learning activity. Oral work includes the student's ability to respond orally to questions which may or may not be related to LIFEPAC activities or any type of oral report assigned by the teacher. The points may then be totaled and a final grade entered along with the date that the LIFEPAC was completed.

The Student Record Book which was specifically designed for use with the Alpha Omega curriculum provides space to record weekly progress for one student over a nine week period as well as a place to post self test and LIFEPAC scores. The Student Record Books are available through the current Alpha Omega catalog; however, unlike the enclosed forms these books are not for duplication and should be purchased in sets of four to cover a full academic year.

WEEKLY LESSON PLANNER

Week of:

	Subject	Subject	Subject	Subject
Monday				
	Subject	Subject	Subject	Subject
Tuesday				
	Subject	Subject	Subject	Subject
Wednesday				
	Subject	Subject	Subject	Subject
Thursday				
	Subject	Subject	Subject	Subject
Friday				

WEEKLY LESSON PLANNER

			Week of:	

	Subject	Subject	Subject	Subject
Monday				
	Subject	Subject	Subject	Subject
Tuesday				
	Subject	Subject	Subject	Subject
Wednesday				
	Subject	Subject	Subject	Subject
Thursday				
	Subject	Subject	Subject	Subject
Friday				

Student Name _____   Year _____

Bible

LP #	Self Test Scores by Sections 1	2	3	4	5	Self Test Points	LIFEPAC Test	Oral Points	Report Points	Final Grade	Date
01											
02											
03											
04											
05											
06											
07											
08											
09											
10											

Language Arts

LP #	Self Test Scores by Sections 1	2	3	4	5	Self Test Points	LIFEPAC Test	Oral Points	Report Points	Final Grade	Date
01											
02											
03											
04											
05											
06											
07											
08											
09											
10											

Mathematics

LP #	Self Test Scores by Sections 1	2	3	4	5	Self Test Points	LIFEPAC Test	Oral Points	Report Points	Final Grade	Date
01											
02											
03											
04											
05											
06											
07											
08											
09											
10											

Student Name _____   Year _____

Science

| LP # | Self Test Scores by Sections | | | | | Self Test Points | LIFEPAC Test | Oral Points | Report Points | Final Grade | Date |
	1	2	3	4	5						
01											
02											
03											
04											
05											
06											
07											
08											
09											
10											

History & Geography

| LP # | Self Test Scores by Sections | | | | | Self Test Points | LIFEPAC Test | Oral Points | Report Points | Final Grade | Date |
	1	2	3	4	5						
01											
02											
03											
04											
05											
06											
07											
08											
09											
10											

Spelling/Electives

| LP # | Self Test Scores by Sections | | | | | Self Test Points | LIFEPAC Test | Oral Points | Report Points | Final Grade | Date |
	1	2	3	4	5						
01											
02											
03											
04											
05											
06											
07											
08											
09											
10											

NOTES

INSTRUCTIONS FOR HISTORY & GEOGRAPHY

The LIFEPAC curriculum from grades two through twelve is structured so that the daily instructional material is written directly into the LIFEPACs. The student is encouraged to read and follow this instructional material in order to develop independent study habits. The teacher should introduce the LIFEPAC to the student, set a required completion schedule, complete teacher checks, be available for questions regarding both content and procedures, administer and grade tests, and develop additional learning activities as desired. Teachers working with several students may schedule their time so that students are assigned to a quiet work activity when it is necessary to spend instructional time with one particular student.

The Teacher Notes section of the Teacher's Guide lists the required or suggested materials for the LIFEPACs and provides additional learning activities for the students. The materials section refers only to LIFEPAC materials and does not include materials which may be needed for the additional activities. Additional learning activities provide a change from the daily school routine, encourage the student's interest in learning and may be used as a reward for good study habits.

ADDITIONAL LEARNING ACTIVITIES

Section I Governments

1. Do a short report (300 words or so) on a colony (Asian, African, South American) of some European country (England, Holland, France, Germany). Why did the European country colonize this place? What kind of products did it gain from the colony? How were the natives of the colony treated? How much self-government did the natives have?

2. Review with the class the idea of their own development as individuals. Who has had the most influence over their lives? How have other groups (school, church, community) influenced them? How much decision and control do they have over their own lives, and how can they exercise that control?

Section II Governments in Our World

1. Do a report, either oral or written, on the religious convictions of one American president and show how that belief influenced his actions as president.

2. Make a chart listing as many of the elected representatives (president, United States senator, United States representative, mayor, legislative representative, etc.) who affect your life as you can think of, listing their offices, their specific duties, and the ways in which they affect your life.

3. Perform a skit in which you show how the life of an average worker is different under capitalistic, socialistic and communistic governments. How much freedom does each worker have? How responsible is he for his own life? How much control does he have over working conditions, living situations, and buying habits?

4. Review with the class the entire idea of how countries make decisions concerning their attitudes toward other countries. What prompts certain countries to make treaties, to go to war, to improve their trade with other countries, and so on?

5. Review with the class the entire concept of authority and the Christian obligation toward all authority-God, family, school, government. When and where does that obligation begin and end? How can we best fulfill that obligation?

Section III Shapers of Political Thought

1. Make a chart (not necessarily a map) showing the most powerful forces in the world in 1600, 1700, 1800, 1900, 1950, and today.

2. Make a list of ten things that you are "free" to do and ten things that you are not free to do. Share your list with a friend who has made a similar list. Decide between yourselves why you are or are not free to do these things.

3. Make a list of ten things that you are obligated to do. Indicate specifically who has obligated you to do these things (God, your parents, government, etc.) and why they obligated you.

4. Discuss with the class whether they think it is ever justifiable (and under what circumstances) to break society's laws. Cite examples such as the American Revolution and the Civil Rights demonstrations of the 1960s as possible examples of cases where laws were purposely broken for motives that later brought good results.

5. Talk about and stress the importance of communication.

ADDITIONAL LEARNING ACTIVITIES

Section I U.S. Constitution and Rights

1. Could you make a case for Biblical education as being an asset to a nation? State it in words and arguments that would convince (and not offend) the non-Christian.

2. What freedoms are expressed in the Bill of Rights of the United States Constitution, and how do they correspond to the responsibilities accompanying them? (For example, what responsibilities accompany the right of free speech?)

3. What laws or actions of government, if any, either in the United States or other countries, might conflict with the laws of God (for example, the repression of freedom of religion in certain governments, laws against family rights in certain countries)?

4. Do a bulletin board showing how the church is free to operate in the United States because of the First Amendment to the United States Constitution (tax-free status for property, freedom to make political statements from the pulpit, etc.).

Section II The Three Branches of Government

1. Let a student do a research project developing a graph showing the relationship of the breakdown in family life to such factors as increase in per-capita income, permissiveness in the media, Supreme Court decisions and so forth.

2. Do you have an opinion about the philosophy on which the Supreme Court ruling against prayer and Bible reading in public schools was based? Have you ever read anything that attempted to prove a cause and effect relationship between the 1962 ruling and the drop in standards and performances in public schools?

Section III Bills and Laws

1. Choose a panel of five to discuss what might have occurred if a compulsory school law had not been passed in 1852.

2. Discuss this question with your class: Could there have been a persistent effort by our government to curb discrimination had there not been a Biblical rooting to our Constitution?

ADDITIONAL LEARNING ACTIVITIES

Section I Political Parties

1. Have two students volunteer to be candidates from opposing parties. Ask them how they stand on (1) lowering taxes, (2) reducing crime, (3) increasing or decreasing welfare, (4) unemployment, (5) the death penalty and other questions the class may have.

2. Divide the class into two groups and take opposing sides on the issue of the importance of politics. Let a third group take the position that it really does not matter because the government will run things anyway.

Section II The Working of Political Parties

1. Do you believe the differences between the major political parties are more fictional than real? Explain. Which of the major parties seems to be the most passionate about its principles? Cite examples.

2. Do you think an independent party could nominate a man for president who would win more votes than the candidate of the major parties? Why or why not?

3. Would you find politics confusing and uninteresting if you lived in a multiparty system? Defend your answer.

4. Do you think that there is a value to the independent party? Explain. Can it influence the policies of the major parties? If so, how?

5. Plan to attend a local political party meeting. Go with the purpose of listening to the issues and acquiring appreciation and respect for the men and women who put their time and energy into this activity.

6. Attempt to evaluate the major positions of both the Democrats and Republicans and then formulate an independent party platform based on parallel Biblical issues.

7. Research the campaign platform of the present administration and seek to determine the degree to which they have been successful in meeting their goals.

8. Initiate a correspondence with one of the independent parties and ask them to provide material indicating the degree of effect they have had on American politics.

9. Discuss these question with your class: Can you conceive of a man running for president of the United States or governor of his state without the backing and support of a political party? Do you agree with the system of political parties? Why or why not?

10. Discuss these question with your class: How important is the local party in terms of national politics? Can the local political party really change things in your area? If so how?

11. If possible, arrange a field trip to the local headquarters of a political party (or during an election campaign, to the headquarters of a candidate) so that students can see how their local political organization works.

Section III Voting

1. Pretend you are running for office. Write up an advertising brochure stating your convictions or write a speech to be given on television. Share with the class. What office would you run for?

2. Discuss these question with your class: Do you believe a nation is better served by a minimum voting age of 18 or 21? Explain.

ADDITIONAL LEARNING ACTIVITIES

3. Discuss these question with your class: How will you proceed to vote? (Assume that you are qualified and have registered in time.) Explain the process from analysis of candidates to the day of election.

4. Put together a mock polling place. Run off ballots and stage a series of brief campaign speeches. Conduct a ballot by secret vote. Afterward, let each student express how he felt in filling out the ballot. Was it too complicated? Why or why not?

5. Invite a voting registrar into class to register those students over eighteen and to tell those under eighteen how to register when they reach that age.

ADDITIONAL LEARNING ACTIVITIES

Section I Ancient Governments

1. Let a student do research on kibbutz, non-Christian commune or Christian community life styles.

2. Write a 200-word paper stating what democracy means to you.

3. Do a bulletin board or map showing the Roman Empire, highlighting especially Palestine and any other predominantly Jewish settlements in the Empire.

Section II Governmental Systems

1. Appoint a student to research a comprehensive study comparing their democratic principles of education with Bible teachings of Christ. Have the student include Scriptural references to validate his work.

2. With a group, look up (in an encyclopedia or other resource book) the specific division of labor in the Middle Ages and an emerging middle class. (For example, the need for a large supply of bread was met by the miller and the baker, and so forth.) Perhaps make a poster or bulletin board showing the variety of different occupations in a typical town of the Middle Ages.

3. Do an oral report on a strong sovereign (Louis XIV, Elizabeth I, Napoleon) or a strong international politician (Bismarck, Disraeli, Kissinger) who built up the economy and security of his or her country through treaties, trade laws and so forth.

4. Do a report, either oral or written, on one of the Jewish revolts against Rome and its effects in terms of further persecutions of the Jews.

5. Do a short report, either oral or written, on the history of Jerusalem under one of the following rules: Hebrew, Roman, Islam, Christian, Israeli.

Section III Dictatorship

1. Make a bulletin board or map that shows the alliances and treaties that led to either World War I or World War II.

2. With a group research a Communist country to discover how and why it handles its relations with other countries. Perhaps if more than one group did this project, the groups could work together to compare their results.

3. With another group, choose and research two countries that have been traditional rivals and adversaries (Germany/France, Russia/China, Israel/Egypt). Prepare a discussion in which you determine how and why these two countries have been rivals and why these rivalries have weakened and harmed (or perhaps helped and strengthened) these two countries.

4. Make a bulletin board showing the basic strategic alignments of the Cold War ("free" Western countries, Communist bloc countries, neutral Third World countries).

5. Discuss with the class the Hebrew phobia of the nineteenth century that eventually led to Hitler's ability to persecute the Jews in the 1930s. How does that kind of phobia happen and how can a thing such as the Jewish Holocaust happen? How can it be prevented from happening again?

ADDITIONAL LEARNING ACTIVITIES

6. Make a bulletin board or map showing the countries that live under democratic, socialistic and communistic governments. You will have to chose a definition of "democratic" for this. Discuss why some nations that call themselves democracies are not.

ADDITIONAL LEARNING ACTIVITIES

Section I Government, Discrimination, American Society

1. All around you are many well adjusted, mature men and women in the business, political, and sports world—many of them without a personal relationship with Jesus. What do you have to say about this situation?

2. Set up a panel show format. Let one team take the role of nonbelievers and a second team the role of Bible-based believers. Let the Moderator (assisted by a team of "experts") present identical situations to the two teams. The situations should be in the realm of opportunities, decisions, temptations, and challenges.

3. Have two students debate the Supreme Court decision of 1962 to ban prayer in the public schools.

4. Do an oral report for the class on some American religious leader who has also influenced governmental laws and policies or helped to change American society in general.

5. Discuss with the class the idea of "prejudice." Starting with the roots of the word—to pre-judge-ask students why and how people are prejudiced against other people and how and why that prejudice should be overcome.

6. Do an oral report on anti-Semitic laws that existed in the United States and other countries even into the twentieth century.

7. Review with the class the concept of discrimination against certain groups in the United States. How did this discrimination come about? How was it circumvented and prevented? How can it be prevented from occurring in the future? Compare this discrimination to that against the Jews throughout history mentioned in Section I.

8. Review with the class the history of discrimination against the Jews. How did it begin? How was it continued and fostered, even by Christians? How can it be prevented today?

Section II "Opinion and Truth" in Politics

1. List ten specific ways in which you as an individual can be a Christian witness for the rest of the world. Give specific examples. Share these examples with the rest of the class.

2. If possible, bring into class a local clergyman (or a group of clergymen) to discuss with the class what he believes his responsibility is in relation to the larger world and how he shows that responsibility. For example: Would he urge his congregation to vote for or against a certain candidate or issue? Would he take a stand in his pulpit on a controversial, public issue?

3. Review with the class the idea of being a good citizen. How can they best fulfill their obligation as Christian citizens? What can they do to make their government (local, state, and federal) closer to the ideal of a godly community?

4. Review with the class how they can be responsible politically as strong Christians. How can they as individuals influence their leaders and public opinion? How can they best exercise their rights and responsibilities as citizens?

ADDITIONAL LEARNING ACTIVITIES

Section III Politics and Propaganda

1. Discuss the following with your class:
   a. Is it always wrong to be on the "bandwagon"?
   b. Is the majority always right? Discuss how it is better to be in the minority and to be right than to be with the crowd and be wrong. (The crowd shouting "Crucify Him" was in the majority, but they were wrong.)
   c. Cite some ways that mass media could be used to uplift the nation morally, spiritually and educationally.
   d. Is it possible to be a Christian and be in politics? If you think so explain how and why it is important for the nation.

2. Plan a field trip to some government-service building (city hall, the court house, the police department, etc.) in order to find out how it works and how you as a citizen can influence that institution.

3. Decide on an important issue affecting you, your family, your church or your school, and write to a public official who is most responsible for affecting that issue, telling him or her of your position on the issue. Make it as convincing and as rational as possible. Perhaps you should show it to your teacher before you mail it to have it checked for spelling, punctuation, sentence structure, grammar and so forth, as well as for the effectiveness of your arguments.

4. Discuss with the class the idea of rumor and unfounded accusations against an entire group. Can the students think of any cases where an entire group has been stereotyped and falsely accused? How? Why? How can such accusation be prevented and avoided?

5. If possible, invite a local leader of a political party into class to advise students on how they can become involved in the political process.

6. Discuss with the students ways in which they can be good citizens besides just voting (for example: becoming involved in local politics, keeping in touch with their elected representatives, etc.).

7. Review with the class the importance of the entire American political system and the necessity of their involvement as voters and citizens in order to exercise a strong Christian influence over society.

ADDITIONAL LEARNING ACTIVITIES

Section I Economic Growth and Free Enterprise

1. With a group of students, devise an imaginary exchange system by which each of you would exchange one of your possessions for someone else's possession. Try to determine exactly how much you consider your possessions to be worth. How much or how little would you trade something for?

2. If possible, visit a local large business or plant with the class, with special emphasis on making the students aware of the division of labor that occurs in such a business.

3. Write a brief report of one businessman (such as John D. Rockefeller, Andrew Carnegie or Bill Gates) or one labor leader (Samuel Gompers, George Meany) who has had a tremendous effect on the economy and industry of this country.

4. Discuss with the class the importance science and technology have played in international relations in terms of speed of communications, speed of travel, new weapons and so forth.

5. Discuss with the class what they think will be the most important inventions or technological innovations of the next twenty-five or fifty years and how these changes will affect them and their way of living.

6. If possible, bring in a newspaper or magazine from ten or twenty-five years ago to show students the rise in prices due to inflation. If possible, bring in magazines or newspapers with many different types of representative prices (for example, food, clothes, automobiles, etc.).

7. Make a chart showing how much one dollar (or $10.00 or $100.00) bought ten or twenty-five years ago and how much less it buys today.

8. Discuss the idea of interdependence (and perhaps balance of payments) by asking students what products in their homes were imported from foreign countries and what products they think are the most heavily exported by the United States.

Section II A Guide to Learning World Financial Terms

1. Make a bulletin board in which you show the medieval land trade routes for Europe or the sea routes of the Age of Exploration.

2. Using an encyclopedia or other reference book, draw a poster or map on which you show the most important products that were brought from the various corners of the world during the Age of Exploration and how they benefited the needs of certain European countries (for example: spices, silk, etc.).

3. Write a report in which you show how a specific European king or queen (Elizabeth I of England, or Louis XIV of France, for example) helped speed the Age of Exploration, the economy of his or her country and generally the use of money and the emergence of the middle class in Europe.

4. Make a bulletin board showing how much the United States dollar is worth in comparison to five other foreign currencies and how much it was worth five, ten and twenty-five years ago.

ADDITIONAL LEARNING ACTIVITIES

5. Discuss with the class the idea of the accumulation wealth and the movement from one "class" in society to another. How easy would it be for one of them to accumulate one million dollars? How would their lives change or stay the same? What could they do with their money that they cannot do now?

Section III International Finance and Currency

1. Write a report about a group of people that still uses the system of exchanging one good for another (for example: a primitive tribe in a remote part of the world, an auctioneer, an antique collector).

2. Make a bulletin board showing as many different mediums of exchange used in the world today as possible, such as barter, gold and silver, coins, paper money, checks and credit cards.

3. Assume you have $50. Follow the international exchange rates once a week for one month. Make a chart tracking the fluctuating value of your $50 against Mexican Pesos, Swiss Francs, Swedish Krona, Japanese Yen, and Israeli New Shekels.

4. Research the "Euro." Discuss which countries have adopted the currency and the reasons behind that decision. Make a chart of the advantages and disadvantages of a world-wide currency.

ADDITIONAL LEARNING ACTIVITIES

Section I Business and the Consumer

1. Make a chart showing how the annual salary for five occupations has gone up in the last five, ten, and twenty-five years.

2. Bring a business person (perhaps the mother or father of one of the students) into the class to talk about the daily problems that he or she faces.

3. Write to a government agency (the Food and Drug Administration, for example) asking them to send you information describing their functions and their regulations or get such information out of your local library or the Internet. Then write a brief report describing their regulations and how they both help and restrict the average consumer and business person.

4. Find out what regulations it takes in your town (for example: zoning restrictions, licensing procedures, etc.) in order to start a specific kind of business. Let the student decide on the type of business.

5. Divide the class into three groups:

    Group One–Decide what advantages a Christian worker has the right to bargain for with his employer (for example higher wages for the good of his family, a vacation with pay, overtime wages, etc.).

    Group Two–Determine how a Christian businessman would bargain with his workers in terms of their needs and his own need and desire for a fair profit. Perhaps the two groups could come together and achieve some kind of a compromise in front of the entire class.

    Group Three–Make a bulletin board on which you show in a pie graph how much profit typical businesses in the United States make (in comparison to their expenses, wages, and so forth).

6. Review with the class how they can be responsible, financially and economically, in their future lives. How can they best prepare themselves for future employment, purchases, property ownership and so on?

Section II Banks and Mergers

1. Write a report in which you demonstrate how the Fed manages the country's money by giving examples of how it has made adjustments in open market operations, discount rates and reserve requirements.

2. Research U.S. government securities such as saving bonds, Treasury bills, notes and bonds. Assume you have $100 to invest. Write a report explaining where you would consider the best place to invest your money.

3. Write the U.S. Treasury. Request a brochure, or film, outlining changes made in the $20 bill first distributed in 1999.

Section III Business Concerns

1. Invite a representative from AT&T® or similar company to the class to talk about how their company has responded to deregulation.

2. As a class research incidences of filed personal bankruptcies over the last 10 years. Make a bulletin board demonstrating your findings. Have a discussion to consider reasons for your findings.

ADDITIONAL LEARNING ACTIVITIES

Section I The History and Workings

1. As a class, subscribe to Barron's® for 3 months. Divide the class into 3 groups. Each week have each group choose one article and report orally to the class as a panel on what the article said and their reaction to it.

2. If possible, invite a stock broker to class. Have them describe to the class the responsibilities involved in their job.

Section II From Choosing to Crashing

1. As a class subscribe to the Wall Street Journal® for one month. Encourage regular reading of articles. At the end of the month have each student write a brief report on what they believe to be the condition of the economy, according to The Wall Street Journal®.

2. Obtain a historical film that explains the Stock Market Crash of 1929. Have the class view the film.

3. Research the Stock Market Crash of 1929 or 1987. Write a report listing the reasons for the crash.

4. Have a class discussion. Consider the impact of the Wall Street Journal® Article "Stocks May Face More Than A Correction." Would the Stock Market Crash have been the same if the article had not been written?

Section III Types and Tracking

1. Have each student assume that they have enough money to purchase 10 shares of stock in a chosen company. Have them track the stock for one month. At the end of the month, have each student prepare a chart tracking the stocks' movement over the course of the month.

2. Make a chart showing 10 representative symbols for each of the following: NYSE®, AMEX®, and NASDAQ®.

ADDITIONAL LEARNING ACTIVITIES

Section I Cash, Credit and Checking Finances

1. Discuss with the class how "free" they are to spend the money they have (through allowances, part-time jobs, etc.). Ask them what restrictions are placed on the spending of that money (by their parents, by others around them, etc.) and how they make choices to determine how they will spend the money.

2. Ask the class the importance of money by asking them exactly how much they think certain amounts ($1.00, $10.00, $100.00, etc.) will buy (i.e., a week's worth of groceries for their family, a decent used car, etc.).

3. Discuss with the class how important they feel hard work is. Is it a desirable end in itself? Is it a means of getting material possessions? Is it a means of satisfaction and enjoyment?

4. Bring in newspaper ads for comparison shopping (for example: advertisements for three or four local grocery stores that show various prices on different products). Use these ads to start a discussion on the idea of comparison shopping and the idea of supply and demand. (Why are prices different at different stores?)

5. In class, plan with the students a budget based on their incomes, their necessities and their desired purchases.

6. Do some comparison shopping of your own. Price an item that you have been very interested in purchasing in at least five different stores (different types of stores, if possible) and bring the results back to class to share with the others.

7. Ask your mother and father to go over the family budget with you to show you how much they must allot for certain fixed expenditures (mortgage, food, etc.) and how much they have left over for savings, miscellaneous items, entertainment, and so forth. Make a pie graph showing how the expenses of your family are divided.

8. Research the laws in your state concerning credit (who can get it, how much interest can be charged, etc.).

Section II Grants, Loans and IRAs

1. If possible, invite a local banker into class to advise the students about how to start savings and checking accounts and about the best ways to establish and use credit.

2. Discuss with the class the idea of budgeting and credit. How can they be responsible for their money? How can they keep within a budget?

3. Invite a representative from a company that provides IRAs. Give a presentation to the class. Discuss the different plans and the risks involved.

Section III Savings, E-Cash and Traveler's Checks

1. Call a few banks in your area. Inquire about E-cash card availability or when E-cash cards might be available. Give an oral report to the class on your findings.

2.   Visit three banks and one SLA. Obtain brochures about their savings accounts. Determine rules, interest rates, fees and penalties for accounts at each of the banks and the SLA. Decide which bank would be the best to begin a savings account with. Write a brief report of findings, decisions made and reasons.

ADDITIONAL LEARNING ACTIVITIES

Section I Euro and International Finance

1.   Choose one city of international finance. Research that city. Write a report expanding on factors which make it a chosen place of international finance.

2.   Create a chart listing ten benefits of the use of the Euro dollar.

3.   Examine the countries involved in the use of the Euro dollar. Choose one country. Create a Euro dollar design that you believe would work well for that country.

Section II U.S. States, Capital Cities and the Global Traveler

1.   Imagine you are a world traveler. Research travel agents, the library and the Internet. Plan your own trip to Norway, India or Japan. Make an itinerary. Create a poster using pictures. Outline plans for your trip.

2.   Invite a travel agent to class. Have them talk about most popular places to visit in the world. Ask them to present their personal favorite world travel hints.

3.   Choose two states. Prepare an oral report listing ten interesting things about each state.

Section III Neighbors, Heroes and the Holy Land

1.   Choose one country other than the United States. Demonstrate interdependence among countries of the world by making a chart showing the major exports and imports of your chosen country, emphasizing what other countries it exports products to and what other countries it imports from.

2.   Bring up the subject of Jewish immigration to other countries (especially the United States) during persecution in other countries. Ask the students why these people emigrated and what freedoms other countries (especially the United States) had to offer.

3.   Make a bulletin board or map showing Israel in relation to its Arab neighbors in the Middle East.

4.   Do an oral report on the series of wars between Israel and the Arab world in the last thirty years (their causes, effects, etc.) and the recent negotiations that led to a settlement between Israel and Egypt.

5.   Do an oral report on the efforts necessary to create the state of Israel in the late 1940s.

6.   Do an oral report on how the three major world religions coexist in Jerusalem today.

ALTERNATE

T
E
S
T
S

Reproducible Tests
for use with the History &
Geography 1200 Teacher's
Guide

Name _____
Date _____
Score _____

True/False (each answer, 2 points).

1. _____ The House of Lords can decide whether a law is in guidelines with the constitution.

2. _____ If you speak of a right-wing party, you are speaking of a group which holds liberal views.

3. _____ Aquinas never did finish *Summa Contra Gentiles*, a treatise which explained Christian theology.

4. _____ Making mass transportation available is one of the ways a local government can assist a citizen.

5. _____ Public utilities include amusement parks and county fairs.

6. _____ The House of Commons is more powerful than the House of Lords.

7. _____ The Senate reviews the laws of the U.S. to make sure they are constitutional.

8. _____ Thomas Aquinas was a writer of the Renaissance period.

Fill in the blanks (each answer, 3 points).

9. Congress can override a presidential veto by _____ majority vote.

10. The _____ is usually the leader in majority party in the House of Commons.

11. The two houses of the U.S. Congress are: _____ and _____ .

12. The two houses of the British Parliament are the: _____ and _____ .

13. Most one-party systems are associated with _____ .

14. The two works that Karl Marx wrote are: _____ and _____ .

15. Paul tells Timothy that even if the leader is corrupt, pray for the leader's _____ so that he may change and run an honorable government.

16. Applying Christian principles in politics such as Daniel did can have an influence in high government, and we find the story of Daniel's stand for the Lord in the book of _____ , chapter number 6.

17. The right to a speedy trial is incorporated in the term _____ .

18. A _____ government passes laws to protect the rights of its citizens.

19.   Discuss the importance of governments.

    _____

    _____

20.   List two ways in which the government helps us.

    _____

    _____

21.   In recent elections in Mexico, the _____ has lost control of Congress for the first time in years.

List five countries with multiparty systems (each answer, 3 points).

22.   _____

23.   _____

24.   _____

25   _____

26.   _____

Match the following types of government with Aristotle's definition of them
(each answer, 2 points).

27.   _____ polity   a.   leader works for the good of the people

28.   _____ monarchy   b.   leader works his own benefit

29.   _____ aristocracy   c.   a few working for the good of the people

30.   _____ democracy   d.   a few working for their own benefit

31.   _____ tyranny   e.   the rule of many for the benefit of all

32.   _____ oligarchy   f.   dangerous mob self rule

Choose one (each answer, 2 points).

33.   Which of these Bible passages instruct us to pray for those in authority?

    _____ Romans 13:1-18

    _____ Psalm 119:1-2

    _____ 1 Timothy 2:1-4

34.   China has what type of government?

    _____ democracy

    _____ communist

    _____ monarchy

83/104

Name _____
Date _____
Score _____

True/False (each answer, 2 points).

1. _____ Both Houses of Congress are part of the legislative branch.

2. _____ A sitting bill is a bill that is inactive in Congress at the moment.

3. _____ If a committee does not act on a bill, it's the same as if they would have voted it down.

4. _____ A bill moves from the House to the White House

5. _____ H.R. signifies a House bill and S. a Senate bill

6. _____ The Tax Court is a court established by Congress.

7. _____ The impeachment process of a federal judge comes only through the Pentagon.

8. _____ The president is in a different branch than the judiciary branch of government.

9. _____ In 1998 the move concerning the impeachment hearings of President Clinton started in the Senate.

10. _____ George Mason refused to sign the Constitution.

Fill in the blanks (each problem, 2 points).

11. If the president doesn't want to deal with a bill and lets it sit for _____ days while Congress is in session, it automatically becomes law.

12. A brief, "first-step" presentation of a work to be completed is called a _____ .

13. Marking up a bill means that the subcommittee might make _____ and add _____ before they recommend a bill to the full committee.

14. Legislation that is under the voting process in the House of Representatives is called a _____ bill.

15. To _____ a new law means to explain the meaning of that law or to clarify the definition of that law.

16. The president has traveled out of the country in order to talk to Germany about export and import agreements. This is known as having _____ .

17. Federal courts even have the right to _____ laws that they feel are violating the Constitution.

18. A _____ is when one party controls the House and another party controls the Senate.

19.   The legislative system is given powers granted to it by the Constitution in _____ .

20.   The Constitution was completed in the year _____ .

21.   A diplomat who resides in a country where he represents his country is called a(n) _____ .

22.   Ensuring _____ means ensuring peacefulness or calmness.

23.   A dentist would apply for a license with the _____ .

24.   If Mr. Johnson takes a case all the way to the Supreme Court concerning his being unlawfully jailed, he is trying to see that a wrong be righted. The word for "correcting a wrong that was done" is _____ .

25.   The assembly called for a "bill of rights" that would list the _____ of the individual American.

26.   The _____ Amendment gives a citizen of the U.S. a right to a speedy trial.

27.   Jurisdiction means the power of _____ .

28.   A bill that becomes law is called _____ .

29.   The _____ guarantees the right to keep and bear arms.

Match these items (each answer, 2 points).

30.   _____   in session   a. listen to various experts about the bill, both supporters and opponents of the bill.

31.   _____   floor session   b. two-thirds majority vote needed.

32.   _____   hearings   c. Activity concerning a bill which may include debates and compromise.

33.   _____   override   d. The time when Congress is active and members are present, fulfilling their respective duties.

Which statement is true? (2 points)

34.   _____   a. A president may be able to ignore the Congressional override of his veto, even if they have enough votes.

        _____   b. Having agencies outside of Washington, D.C. helps fight the "Beltway mentality."

        _____   c. Discussing and even arguing over a legislation is called ordering a bill reported.

        _____   d. A standing bill is one that has been passed as a law.

Put a check beside all of the offices underneath the jurisdiction of the executive office (each answer, 2 points).

35. _____ a. National House of Senatorial Privilege

     _____ b. National Security Council

     _____ c. Office of Policy Development

     _____ d. The Overview Chamber

Match these items (each answer, 2 points).

36. _____ president   a. negate, destroy

37. _____ statutory construction   b. guideline document in judicial review

38. _____ nullify   c. chosen, appointed

39. _____ Constitution   d. head of armed forces

40. _____ nominated   e. interprets the meaning of laws and administrative rules and regulations

41. _____ Article III of the Constitution   f. gives power to the judicial system of courts

Match these items (each answer, 2 points).

42. _____ 39   a. number of delegates who signed the Constitution

43. _____ 100   b. number of senators in Senate

44. _____ 435   c. number of representatives in House

Match the phrases that best fit each other (each answer, 2 points).

45. _____ George Washington   a. president is part of this branch

46. _____ petition   b. trading with each other, printing state currency

47. _____ Ben Franklin   c. a request

48. _____ reason for not signing   d. a signer of the Constitution

49. _____ problems between the states   e. presided over the Constitutional Convention

50. _____ executive   f. "too much power given to the federal government."

Mark the phrase(s) below which is/are true concerning the Constitution. (2 points)

51. _____ The right to peaceably assemble is found in the First Amendment.

     _____ The Second Amendment says that Congress may not prevent a religion from free exercise.

     _____ The fist ten Amendments to the Constitution are called the Bill of Rights.

     _____ The Tenth Amendment gives states certain freedoms and control.

     _____ The Third Amendment includes the freedom of speech and freedom of press.

History & Geography 1203 Alternate Test

Name _____
Date _____
Score _____

Fill in the blanks (each problem, 2 points).

1.   Three countries with two-party systems include _____ , _____ , _____ .

2.   Name six Democratic presidents. _____ , _____ , _____ , _____ , _____ , _____ .

3.   During the first three presidential elections the _____ chose the president and the vice president.

4.   The two major parties in Great Britain are the Labor and _____ parties.

5.   The headquarters for both major parties are located in _____ .

6.   In the 1860 presidential election the Democratic Party ran two candidates, _____ and _____ .

7.   Name five third parties listed: _____ , _____ , _____ , _____ , _____ .

8.   The Prohibition Party was founded in 1869 solely for the purpose of preventing the manufacturer and sale of alcoholic beverages in the United States. The Prohibition Party is an example of _____ .

9.   The _____ believed in a loose construction of the Constitution.

10.   The Anti-Federalists believed in a _____ of the Constitution.

11.   The parties have to depend largely on _____ for their campaign funding.

12.   The Republican National Committee publishes a monthly digest of information for Republicans called _____ .

13.   In an Australian ballot, the names of all candidates appear on a _____ ballot.

14.   The average number of voters per precinct is _____ .

15.   Nearly all states allow those who are absent on _____ to vote.

16.   In absentee voting, a person marks the ballot and then swears before a _____ that he is a registered and qualified voter. He then sends his ballot to the county _____ .

17.   The alternative to voting a straight ticket is to vote a _____ .

18.   One way to cut down on the number of elections is to not have an election when all the persons running are _____ , which happens frequently.

19.   A _____ is the submitting of a proposed public measure for voting by the general public.

True/False (each answer, 2 points).

20. _____ Under Dwight D. Eisenhower, the Republican Party would be in office from 1952 through 1972.

21. _____ A group that may not be in agreement with the general direction of the larger population is called a faction.

22. _____ A provision is arrangement or groundwork laid to create worker unrest.

23. _____ A challenger is a person who does not hold an office but who is trying to unseat an incumbent.

24. _____ The Bull Moose Party was formed by Theodore Roosevelt in 1912.

25. _____ The Republicans have never controlled both the House of Representatives and the Senate at the same time.

26. _____ The Democrats won the presidency in 1976, 1980 and 1996.

27. _____ Planks are parts of the party platform in the form of issues that are presented to the people. Civil rights, taxes and energy are a few examples of the issues.

28. _____ Both the Democratic and Republican parties have a state committee in each state.

29. _____ In state elections, only the governor, lieutenant governor and members of the state legislature would be elected under the short-ballot system.

Mark the two 1860 presidential candidates for the Democrats (each answer, 2 points).

30. _____ a. Stephen Douglas
    _____ b. Abraham Lincoln
    _____ c. Franklin Pierce
    _____ d. John Breckinridge
    _____ e. James Buchanan
    _____ f. Adlai Stevenson

Ross Perot formed the (2 points)

31. _____ a. United We Stand Party.
    _____ b. American Party.
    _____ c. Prohibition Party.

Which was NOT true about the Alien and Sedition Act? (each answer, 2 points)

32. _____ a. The president was given power to deport any alien he deemed dangerous.
    _____ b. The president could give asylum to any immigrant he wished.
    _____ c. The president could imprison any editor who criticized him for his actions.

History & Geography 1203 Alternate Test

Match the words with their definitions (each answer, 2 points).

33. _____ Republican Party
34. _____ loose construction
35. _____ Constitutional Convention
36. _____ Andrew Jackson
37. _____ strict construction
38. _____ Abraham Lincoln

a. limits the government to the powers which the Constitution delegated to it.
b. gathering for the purpose of creating a Constitution which laid down the laws for running the U.S.
c. Republican president during the Civil War.
d. began as a series of anti-slavery political meetings held in the Midwest in 1854.
e. free interpretation of the Constitution, allowing the government all powers not denied it.
f. started the Democratic Party.

Mark the sentences that are TRUE (each answer, 2 points).

39. _____ a. The Democrats blamed the Republicans for the Stock Market crash of 1929.
_____ b. The Democrats won the Presidency in the 90s but lost control of the Congress.
_____ c. The Democratic party is the oldest political party in the United States.
_____ d. The Anti-Federalists were one of the first two American political parties; they wanted a strong central government.
_____ e. The "Era of Good feelings" was a period from 1816-1824 where there was only one political party: the Democrat-Republicans.

Match these items (each answer, 2 points).

40. _____ Thomas Jefferson
41. _____ John Adams
42. _____ Alexander Hamilton
43. _____ George Washington

a. Secretary of the Treasury
b. first president
c. second president
d. third president

Matching (each answer, 2 points).

44. _____ Dwight D. Eisenhower
45. _____ Jimmy Carter
46. _____ Bull Moose Party
47. _____ United We Stand Party
48. _____ coalition

a. formed by Theodore Roosevelt in 1912.
b. Republican president.
c. temporary alliance of political parties.
d. Democratic president.
e. formed by Ross Perot in 1992.

Mark the sentences that are true (each answer, 2 points).

49. _____ a. The Republican Party began as a series of anti-slavery political meetings held in the midwest in 1854.
_____ b. During the election of 1824, Andrew Jackson won the most electoral votes, but not the majority needed to be elected president.
_____ c. The Anti-Federalist wanted to limit the federal government strictly to the powers the constitution delegated to it.
_____ d. Third parties play an important role in the strengthening the two major parties.
_____ e. If a political party puts people above the needs of its party it is known as partisan politics.

Who was praised for his efforts in the Persian Gulf War, but was criticized for his poor efforts in strengthening the nation's economy? (2 points)

50. _____ a. Bill Clinton

_____ b. George Bush, Sr.

_____ c. Ronald Reagan

Which is a FALSE statement? (2 points)

51. _____ There are generally between 3 to 5 election officers at each polling place.

_____ A primary is an early election in which delegates select and nominate candidates for office.

_____ George Bush was once vice president under Ronald Reagan.

_____ the caucus assures absolute secrecy

Match the words with their definitions (each answer, 2 points).

52. _____ short ballot

53. _____ election officers

54. _____ inspectors and judges

55. _____ office bloc agreement

56. _____ a criticism of elections

a. responsible for the proper conduct of the election

b. used to elect the president, vice president, and members of Congress

c. chosen by the election board

d. national, state, and local elections come on the same day

e. titles of offices appear across the ballot, candidates of both part

Mark the sentences that are TRUE (each answer, 2 points).

57. _____ a. A contested election means that the losing candidate calls for a recount.

_____ b. A fire station is an acceptable building used for a polling place.

_____ c. A church is an acceptable building used for a polling place.

_____ d. A local hamburger restaurant is an acceptable building used for a polling place.

_____ e. A library is an acceptable building used for a polling place.

Name _____
Date _____
Score _____

Answer *true* **or** *false* (each answer, 2 points).

1. _____ The colony was actually a group of people settled in a particular area who carry the same interests.

2. _____ The rivalries between the city-states had no redeeming value whatsoever.

3. _____ The plebeians were upper-class citizens.

4. _____ Feudalism started in Northern Europe and spread throughout the continent, but was strongest in England.

5. _____ The Bible book of Judges tells us about the leadership of Gideon.

6. _____ An elected leader in a parliamentary democracy is called a prime minister.

7. _____ Fascism is usually an agreement between three or more political parties.

8. _____ During World War II, Germany was an Allied power.

9. _____ The first opportunity for the Nazi movement came after World War II.

Complete the following statements (each answer, 3 points).

10. To obtain political rights, plebeians formed their own assembly, _____ .

11. The beginnings of democracy were seen in _____ a little more than 400 years before Jesus walked the streets of Jerusalem.

12. *Nobles* overthrew most of the city-state monarchs by _____ .

13. At first the details of procedure of the Twelve Tables were restricted to a body of _____ leaders.

14. In exchange for land, a knight agrees to be a sort of sub-vassal to a vassal. This agreement was known as _____ .

15. The leadership of a _____ is submissive to God's or a god's accountability.

16. A caliph is a supreme leader of the Islamic community and successor of the Prophet _____ .

17. In the late 1970s Jim Jones tried to institute a theocracy, but his abuse of the Bible only led the people of his community into _____ .

18. The four powerful pillars of democracy are: _____ , _____ , _____ , and _____ .

19. One of the prime examples of a fascist government is that of the Italy during World War _____ .

20.   Nazi secret police were known as the _____ .

21.   The _____ was a worldwide result of the stock market panic of the late 1920s.

Match each word with its correct definition (each answer, 2 points).

22.   _____ Pittsburgh

23.   _____ Greek culture

24.   _____ Rome

25.   _____ Sparta

26.   _____ "direct democracy"

27.   _____ Solon

a. civilization that fell due to what many believe was due to a lack of goals

b. example of a city which was founded as a fort with safety in mind

c. the birth of democracy

d. In 594 B.C. he was chosen as an Athenian statesman with reformation powers

e. main strength was its army

f. first name given to the Greek democracy

Match each word with its correct definition (each answer, 2 points).

28.   _____ Hannibal

29.   _____ patricians

30.   _____ accountable

31.   _____ sustenance

32.   _____ 450 B.C.

33.   _____ Feudalism

34.   _____ King John

35.   _____ Cleisthenes

a.   being answerable to others

b.   members of Rome's richest and most important families

c.   leader of the Carthaginians

d.   The Romans' first code of law was established

e.   food and drink; necessary foods in order to stay alive

f.   ruled England in the 1200s

g.   a system of cooperation among peoples which was basically an exchange of land for protection

h.   wrote the proposal that opened up the voting rights to all free adult men in 508 B.C.

Match each word with its correct definition (each answer, 2 points).

36.   _____ Sharia

37.   _____ term

38.   _____ Bangladesh

39.   _____ Josephus

40.   _____ freedom of worship

41.   _____ chancellor

a.   the religious and moral principles of Islam

b.   a Jewish historian who lived shortly after Jesus walked the earth

c.   created a parliamentary democracy in 1991, headed by a prime minister

d.   an assigned period of time for an elected official

e.   not allowed in fascism

f.   the head of state in some forms of government

Place a check by the correct answers (each answer, 2 points).

42.   Which five of these are the essential pillars to creating a government?

     a. _____   Food should be grown within the government's borders.

     b. _____   Leadership is needed.

     c. _____   A standing army should be ready.

     d. _____   Safety is a priority.

     e. _____   The government should have a goal.

     f. _____   The government should assist in trade.

     g. _____   Production must increase every day.

     h. _____   Production and sustenance must be provided daily.

     i. _____   Law and order should be maintained.

     j. _____   Boundary lines must be drawn.

Mark each statement that is NOT true (each answer, 2 points).

43.   a. _____   Tyrants were power-hungry militants who grabbed absolute control by popular vote.

     b. _____   Nobles were lofty, financially well-to-do citizens who carried much power within the community.

     c. _____   Solon established a law which prohibited enslaving people in debt.

44.   a. _____   A fief is the troop of knights granted to the vassal.

     b. _____   King John of England was a vassal himself who refused some of the rulings of Philip and was broke out between the factions.

     c. _____   Subinfeudation is a layering of responsibility.

Choose the answer that is a TRUE statement (each answer, 2 points).

45. a. _____ A dominating nation with extensive territories and a powerful ruler such as Rome's is known as an empire.

    b. _____ The Roman Republic was also known as a socialist government.

    c. _____ The Romans' first code of law was established around 200 B.C.

    d. _____ The Roman Republic lasted over 1000 years.

46. a. _____ The term "ascribing" is the work of writing on parchment.

    b. _____ Theocracy is the rule of the people.

    c. _____ A vassal could buy out his lord.

    d. _____ The system of cooperation known as feudalism ended around the 15th century.

    e. _____ King Richard was a king who later became a knight before going bankrupt.

Mark the statements which are TRUE. (each answer, 2 points)

47. The difference between the Roman republic and the Greek democracy was that:

    a. _____ In Rome, only men with money and property could vote.

    b. _____ In Greece all women were allowed to vote.

    c. _____ In the Roman Senate, the most powerful part of the government, all senators were patricians.

    d. _____ In the Greek government, retired soldiers were given automatic seats in the Senate.

Write the letter of the correct answer on the blank (each answer, 2 points).

48. A ceremony where men become vassals in a lord's manor is called _____ .

    a. empowerment

    b. homage

    c. vassalage

Answer the following question. (5 points)

49. Describe the parts of the medieval court system which are still used in our American court system today.

    _____

    _____

    _____

    _____ .

83/113

Name _____
Date _____
Score _____

Answer *true* or *false* (each answer, 2 points).

1. _____ Public opinion is of no value when the people who hold an opinion voice their opinion.

2. _____ Headlines are sometimes misleading because it is impossible to tell the whole truth in only a few words.

3. _____ Sitcom programs deal with problems of special significance and often mobilize public opinion to support needed reforms.

4. _____ The Alabama Freethought Association was one of the groups who fought the decision allowing the Ten Commandments to be displayed in Judge Roy Moore's courtroom.

5. _____ President Kennedy's administration was known for promoting civil rights.

6. _____ The ancient Rome race was the determining factor of slavery.

7. _____ At the time when Paul was writing his Epistles, many slaves were becoming Christians.

8. _____ Civics is a good course that a young person should study to prepare himself for a career in political science.

9. _____ When a candidate says "everyone on the city police force and the county school board recommend me," the speaker is using testimonials.

10. _____ One of the American Legion programs that young people can take part in their state is called "Young Democrats."

Place a check by the correct statements (each answer, 2 points).

11. a. _____ To be unfair in judgment; to be prejudiced and show partiality is discrimination.

    b. _____ In 1870 the 13th Amendment gave all male citizens the right to vote.

    c. _____ Compulsory separation of a race is called integration.

    d. _____ A group of people that share a distinctive race, culture, heritage, or nationality is called an ethnic group.

Match each word to its correct definition (each answer, 2 points).

12. _____ Philippians 2:3   a. runaway slave who became a Christian

13. _____ Galatians 3:28-29   b. nickname for the U.S., because of the country's ethnic diversity

14. _____ Everett Hale   c. deals with the discrimination of rich over the poor

15. _____ compromise   d. art of coming to an agreement by mutual concession

16. _____ public opinion polls   e. a thorough cleaning out; a purifying

17. _____ purging   f. determine the popularity of the individual as well as government policies

18. _____ James 2:1-9   g. "I am only one, but I am one. What I can do, I should do and, with the help of God, I will do."

19. _____ "the Great Melting Pot"   h. Bible passage that tells us we are one in Christ.

20. _____ Onesimus   i. Bible passage which tells us to prefer others more than ourselves

Match each word with its correct definition (each answer, 2 points).

21. _____ campaign debt   a. established in parishes

22. _____ conscientious   b. a prayer; usually given at the opening of a meeting or event

23. _____ Jackson Day Dinner   c. having diverse human thinking, beliefs and backgrounds within a society

24. _____ glittering generalities   d. involved in provoking the "school prayer issue" ruling of 1962

25. _____ testimonials   e. good Biblical political leaders

26. _____ David and Moses   f. fund-raising dinner held each year by the Democratic party

27. _____ multi-cultural   g. following one's Godly principles

28. _____ invocation   h. "All of these Hollywood stars say that you should Vote for Governor Tibbet."

29. _____ parochial schools   i. deficit incurred due to the expenses of a political effort

30. _____ Madelyn Murray O'Hare   j. using wide-spread universal terms that do not deal with the specific issues at hand

Write the letter of the correct answer on the blanks (each answer, 2 points).

31. Write the letter on the blank beside each opinion marker that affects us.

   a. _____ newspapers

   b. _____ movies

   c. _____ magazines

   d. _____ propaganda

   e. _____ dictionaries

   f. _____ television

   g. _____ radio

Write the letter of the correct answer on the blank (each answer, 2 points).

32. "Thou shalt love thy neighbor as thyself." This verse is found in _____ .

   a. Titus 3:5

   b. Galatians 5:14

   c. Ephesians 2:8,9

   d. Revelation 20:15

   e. Psalm 119:4

33.   What happened in 1890 concerning civil rights? _____

      a.   Twenty states passed laws making it illegal to discriminate a person because of their race

      b.   Twenty states passed laws that made segregation illegal

      c.   Twenty states passed laws that enacted segregation laws

      d.   the formation of the Ku Klux Klan

Complete the following statements (each answer, 2 points).

34.   From looking back at the roots of their beliefs, an easy way to define conservatives and liberals is by saying conservatives want to _____ the good things that have made our country great. Liberals want to _____ the nation from the bad things that would make it suffer.

35.   "Fourscore and seven years ago our _____ brought forth upon this _____ a new nation, conceived in liberty, and dedicated to the proposition that all men are created equal…"-Abraham Lincoln.

36.   Public opinion is a group opinion of individuals on a _____ .

37.   The two research organizations mentioned in the text are Harris and _____ .

38.   Jesus warned us about being deceived by false teachers in _____ .

39.   News commentators might be called _____ on the air.

40.   Two programs that interview persons who are in the political headlines are "Face the Nation" and _____ .

41.   In 1947 public aid for _____ was declared unlawful.

42.   _____ tells us, "For there is no difference between the Jew and the Greek: for the same Lord over all is rich unto all that call upon him."

43.   A good definition of discrimination is a practice that treats equal people unequally nor does it let them have the same opportunities to complete for _____ .

44.   According to 1 John 4:7-8, what is the solution to prejudice? _____

45.   Projecting an image of being one of the common people is called the _____ type of propaganda.

Answer the following question (5 points).

46.   According to Philippians 2:3, how are we to treat each other? _____

_____

_____

_____

_____

114 / 142

Name _____
Date _____
Score _____

Match each word with its correct definition (each answer, 2 points).

1. _____ Adam Smith

a. South African diamond mining companies use some of the diamonds they have mined in their drills bits

2. _____ Karl Marx

b. When businesses battle for the consumer's purchasing choices

3. _____ Proverbs 31

c. where you get money sent back to you after you send in a requirement, like the UPC symbol

4. _____ picket

d. monetary units that were a strong universal standard in the Middle Ages

5. _____ serf

e. a member of feudal class of people in Europe who were owned by heads of the estates where they worked

6. _____ closed shop

f. to encircle a plant or block a plant entrance with unionists carrying signs or placecards expressing their concerns

7. _____ gold coinage

g. a workplace where only union members may be hired

8. _____ rebate

h. the Scottish economist who wrote of the need for basic economic freedoms

9. _____ capital good

i. honors the mother who shops carefully

10. _____ competition

j. wrote the "Communist Manifesto"

Match each word with its correct meaning (each answer, 2 points).

11. _____ circulation

a. Israeli unit of money

12. _____ bank note reporters

b. exchange for goods without the use of money

13. _____ euro

c. things that are grown, mined, or manufactured

14. _____ IMF

d. German unit of money before the euro

15. _____ mark

e. sort of a "United Nations of Financial Diplomacy"

16. _____ goods

f. common European currency

17. _____ barter

g. 1800s era publications which were printed and passed out to help people identify counterfeits

18. _____ First Bank of the United States

h. the moving of money throughout the country, from business to business and person to person

19. _____ shekel

i. started in 1791

Complete the following statements (each answer, 2 points).

20. Descendants of the expelled Russian Mennonite farmers have continued to grow enormous crops of red _____ in the United States.

21. The lower the demand, the _____ a price can be put on the item.

22. Inflation is when an economic condition in which the _____ supply is increasing faster than the supply of goods and services.

61

23. Labor demands a higher wage to compensate for inflation, which leads to higher prices, then even higher wages. This is called a _____ .

24. States began to pass laws, called right-to-_____ laws, banning the union shop.

25. Between 1952 and 1955, Walter Reuther of the _____ and George Meany of the _____ negotiated a merger of the two organizations: the AFL-CIO.

26. A _____ is a good that all people would accept as a means of payment.

27. Who was the "father of economics"? _____

28. The age of _____ helped set the stage for the development of the free market economy in Western Europe and in America.

29. A strategy used to entice the consumer to make a purchase is called a _____ .

30. The _____ is the unit of currency in Japan.

31. _____ is the slang term for dollar bills, because of the green ink used to print the money.

32. The Free Banking Era was in the _____ .

33. Some of the Federal Reserve System's duties include: _____ monetary policy, regulation of _____ and issuing of _____ .

Answer *true* **or** *false* (each answer, 2 points).

34. _____ Inflation is when prices in a national economy increase or the purchasing power of the dollar weakens on a continual basis.

35. _____ Lazer Supermarket increases prices on an item from 75 cents to $1.50, and nobody cares. They buy it anyway. This is an example of inflation.

36. _____ Inflation leads to uncertainty and confusion about prices. It interferes with planning for the future.

37. _____ An important point of building an economy is to see what communications are available.

38. _____ The capitalistic system is also called a free enterprise system.

39. _____ A farmer's market is an example of capitalism at work.

40. _____ Some things to consider in making an economy grow are the labor force and the technology available.

41. _____ Economics can be best defined as being the science of producing, distributing and consuming goods or products.

42. _____ Laws which regulate or curtail business monopolies or dominant financial organizations are called anti-trust laws.

43. _____ Unions have been getting significantly stronger in the past decades.

44. _____ In medieval times, gold was accepted as the universal exchange.

45. _____ Diaz rounded the Cape of Good Hope in 1501.

46. _____ Any bank in the U.S. could have their own paper money during the Free Banking Era.

47. _____ The Federal Central System is the central banking system of the United States.

48. _____ A U.S. "war-time" money was once printed that was good only in Japan.

49. _____ The International Monetary Fund, or IMF, assists nations in their international financial business.

50. _____ An exchange rate is the price of one country's trading status as compared to another country's.

Mark the statements that are true (each answer, 2 points).

51.   a. _____   Your nation's money is considered part of your nation's capital.

     b. _____   Your nation's labor force includes people who want to work but do not have a job at the moment.

     c. _____   Technology means the type of natural resources that are available.

     d. _____   It would not make sense to force an unskilled laborer to work in a surgical position.

     e. _____   Careful study and review is known as capital.

52.   a. _____   Most knights were hiring vassals to run their farming communities.

     b. _____   The religious Reformation helped the increase of trade.

     c. _____   Trade was a reason for the Age of Exploration.

     d. _____   In the 9th and 10th centuries, Europe was a mass of small duchies and provinces.

Mark the following statement(s) that are NOT true (each answer, 2 points).

53.   a. _____   Your nation's capital is your nation's money.

     b. _____   Your nation's capital is your country's tractor equipment.

     c. _____   Your nation's capital is your country's seed business in Missouri.

     d. _____   Your nation's capital is your nation's shoe factory.

     e. _____   Your nation's capital is your neighboring country's money.

Mark the correct answer(s) for the following (each answer, 2 points).

54.   Which of these are "service" jobs?

     a. _____   stationery shop

     b. _____   shoeshiner

     c. _____   nurse

     d. _____   housecleaning

     e. _____   paint salesman

     f. _____   painter

     g. _____   butler

     h. _____   accountant

     i. _____   mathematician

     j. _____   dentist

55.   Mark three types of economic systems.

     a. _____   communism

     b. _____   free agency

     c. _____   mixed company

     d. _____   subscription

     e. _____   capitalistic

     f. _____   cable-line

     g. _____   currency

56.   The Crusades had whetted the European appetite for Eastern goods. When were the Crusades?

     a. _____   (ca. 995–1009)

     b. _____   (ca. 1095–1204)

History & Geography 1207 Alternate Test

140 / 177

Name ____________________
Date ____________________
Score ____________________

Matching (each answer, 2 points).

1. _______ mega-merger
2. _______ Sherman Antitrust Act, 1890
3. _______ price-setting standard
4. _______ proponents
5. _______ open-market operations
6. _______ monopoly
7. _______ The Federal Reserve

a. no rivals or competitors in the marketplace
b. rules on applications from banks who want to merge
c. the purchase or sale of government securities, increasing or decreasing amount of money banks lend
d. guidelines for controlling costs and expenditures by the consumer
e. those that are in support of something
f. a huge union of large corporations or utilities
g. anti-monopoly act awarded victim of a monopoly three times amount his business lost

Fill in the blanks (each answer, 2 points).

8. The actual money's worth for buying products is called ________________________.
9. In 1914 the ________________________ prevented a merging of corporations to have intertwined boards of directors.
10. One of the largest ____________________ in American history occurred when the U.S. Government ruled that the AT&T® Corporation was a monopoly that must be divided so that the telephone market might be more competitive.
11. After the trusts had eliminated the competition, they would cut back on production and ____________________.

Matching (each answer, 2 points).

12. _______ consumer protection law
13. _______ reserve requirements
14. _______ discount rate
15. _______ government securities

a. a governmental regulation; a mandate which is instituted to safeguard the purchaser
b. amount of money the Fed needs to have as a balance
c. Fed Reserve-set interest rate to determine the amount needed to pay back the loan.
d. a government investment in businesses, guaranteeing repayment

Fill in the blanks (each answer, 2 points).

16. Week by week the finances in this country can change, so the selling and buying of ____________________ helps maintain equilibrium.
17. The Federal Reserve System has the authority to expand ____________________ in case of a national emergency, set limits on the ____________________ and manage America's supply of money.
18. The Fed is a(n) ____________________ agency of the United States government.
19. One way to save at the supermarket is to get information on sales. You can do this by looking in newspaper ads, TV or radio commercials or even the ____________________.

Matching (each answer, 2 points).

20. _____ trust

21. _____ Clayton Antitrust Act

22. _____ ethic

23. _____ inflation

24. _____ regulations

25. _____ contract

26. _____ compensate

27. _____ fire codes

28. _____ wage-price spiral

29. _____ Caveat Emptor

30. _____ return policy

a. legally binding written agreement between purchaser and seller

b. wage increases that compete with higher consumer prices in an ever-escalating upturn

c. to make payment to; to financially award a person

d. specifications and safety measures required for buildings

e. a continuing increase in prices and weakening of the purchasing power of money

f. restrictions and rules governing business conduct

g. a principle or value

h. unofficial mergers formed to control prices and production in the marketplace

i. 1914 legislation that dealt against monopolies, particularly in the area of price-fixing

j. a product may be brought back by the purchaser to the seller for an exchange

k. "Let the buyer beware"

Essay: (5 points)

31.   What are some of the ways can you save money when it comes to cars?

_____

_____

_____

_____

_____.

Fill in the blanks (each answer, 2 points).

32.   After Christmas is a time when the businesses wish to move a lot of _____ and ready themselves for the next sales season.

33.   An important part of a Christian's obligation as management is to be fair to his workers. "Thou shalt not defraud thy neighbor, neither _____ him: the wages of him that is hired shall not abide with thee all night until the morning" (_____ 19:13).

34.   The test of good entrepreneurial decision is if there is a recognizable _____ .

35.   In a corporation, the manager is a _____ between his employees and top management.

36.   The chief principle in the Biblical passages Leviticus 19:13 and Deuteronomy 24:14-15 on management is _____ .

37.   Most regulations have to do with the _____ of the individual who may be a customer of the business, or a worker within the business.

38.   The Securities and Exchange Commission regulates the _____ .

39.   The purpose of deregulation is to open up the doors of competition to many businesses in order to offer consumers greater choice in _____ services or products, to lower rates, and to encourage _____ through competition.

40.   The California customer, instead of being held to paying the one price that a utility would force him to pay, now has his choice between Pacific Gas and Electric®, San Diego Gas and Electric®, Southern California Edison®, and _____ other utilities throughout the state.

Matching (each answer, 2 points).

41.   _____ financial obligation

42.   _____ lien

43.   _____ unsecured debt

44.   _____ secured debt

45.   _____ AT&T®

a. was broken up into one long-distance company and seven "Baby Bells" to provide local service

b. the responsibility to pay debts and due notes

c. the right to take, sell or hold property as security or payment of a debt

d. obligation to pay to another a certain amount of money which has collateral that the creditor may seize

e. a promise or obligation to pay to another a certain amount of money which has no collateral

Fill in the blanks (each answer, 2 points).

46.   The exhortation by Paul to "owe no man anything," meaning that _____ is not pleasing to the Lord.

47.   "But if any _____ , and specially for those of his own house, he hath denied the faith, and is worse than an _____ ."

48.   Some monopolies are not functioning to drive prices up and competitors out; they serve the public. An example is the _____ .

49.   About _____ of the checks written in the U.S. are processed by the 20 Federal Reserve Banks.

Matching (each answer, 2 points).

50.   _____ merger

51.   _____ The Fed Banks

a. distribute the cash to financial institutions

b. the combining of two or more corporations or businesses

True/False (each answer, 2 points).

52. _____ When banks borrow money from a Federal Reserve Bank, they are given a certain interest rate to pay back the loan. If the Federal Reserve System raises the rate of interest, the banks will find it harder to make loans.

53. _____ The Fed works to keep the balance of financial strength at a good level by keeping interest rates low in recessions and letting them rise in economic "boom" times.

54. _____ The end-of-year White Sale is a sale on office supplies.

55. _____ In getting a rebate, the original receipt may be required.

56. _____ Walt's fellow workers are going on strike since the price of food has increased dramatically within the last 14 months. They are looking to get a higher salary. This continual rise in salary and consumer goods prices is known as a wage-price spiral.

57. _____ Inflation = More money + Fewer goods.

58. _____ The Airline Deregulation Act was put into effect in 1988.

Select the five dangers of a monopoly (each answer, 2 points).

59. _____ Higher prices.

_____ No rival competition or alternative markets.

_____ Lower quality

_____ Limitation or elimination of certain goods

_____ Smaller workloads

_____ Poor service and attitude

_____ Fewer employees

Check the sentences that are TRUE (each answer, 2 points).

60. _____ The U.S. Treasury, through its Bureau of the Mint and Bureau of Engraving and Printing, produces the nation's dollar and coin supply.

_____ In 1911 the U.S. Postal Service was broken into 3 separate departments.

_____ The Fed issues the nation's coin and paper currency.

_____ Trusts were unofficial mergers formed to control prices and production in the marketplace.

_____ Some monopolies are good.

_____ The Interstate Commerce Commission polices monopolistic practices.

Which of the following statements are TRUE? (each answer, 2 points)

61. _____ California was the first state to undertake the restructuring of the electric utility industry on a state-wide basis.

_____ Deregulation is about increasing rates and reducing supplies.

_____ After passage of the 1996 deregulation law the Baby Bells started merging with each other, and two of them attempted to re-merge into AT&T®.

_____ A lone utility company, Detroit Edison and Consumers Power, faced new competition as deregulation gave people a choice between utility companies. The company tried to battle the act by asking for funds to cover "stranded costs" and lost income once the process was under way, but the deregulation went through.

_____ Those that are in support of something are called its proponents.

The false advertising problem concerning a food manufacturer was that (2 points).

62. _____ The business actually guaranteed satisfaction - and cheapened the product.

_____ The business actually added less to the box - and kept the price the same.

_____ The business actually increased the size of the box - and raised the price of the box.

What is operational management? (each answer, 2 points)

63. _____ making decisions that affect the future of a business

_____ the day to day operation of a business

_____ risk-taking

Which answer(s) is/are NOT TRUE? (2 points)

64. _____ At the local level, businesses must meet building standards.

_____ At the local level, businesses must meet fire codes.

_____ At the local level, businesses must meet zoning laws.

_____ At the local level, businesses must meet government-set billing rates.

_____ At the state level, some businesses must meet licensing.

Mark the sentences that are TRUE (each answer, 2 points).

65. _____ The Federal Communications Commission regulates radio and television to the extent of licensing stations and policing programming.

_____ The National Labor Relations Board regulates and oversees television practices.

_____ The Federal Aviation Administration regulates the airlines.

_____ The Federal Trade Commission regulates all newspapers.

_____ The Securities and Exchange Commission regulates the stock market.

_____ The Federal Reserve Board regulates the postal system.

_____ The Interstate Commerce Commission polices monopolistic practices.

_____ The Food and Drug Administration assesses all foods and drugs consumed.

Which of these statements are TRUE? (each answer, 2 points)

66. _____ Deregulated Investor Owned Utilities are known as IOUs.

_____ The Marshall Plan was an anti-monopoly act which awarded the victim of a monopoly three times the amount that his business lost.

_____ In deregulation, government tightens controls and won't allow other companies to enter the market.

Check the sentences that are TRUE (each answer, 2 points).

67. _____ A Chapter 11 bankruptcy is known as a "straight liquidation."

_____ In a Chapter 13 proceeding, the debtor surrenders their nonexempt property for division among their creditors.

_____ Financial responsibility in the home is found in the Bible passage of 1 Timothy 5:8.

_____ A Chapter 13 bankruptcy filing is called a reorganization.

_____ Monopolies are judged by how strong the competition is between the companies.

_____ In 1971, the Standard Oil Company was divided into more than 30 separate companies.

Which answer is TRUE? (2 points)

68. _____ The U.S. Department of Interior, through its Bureau of the Mint and Bureau of Engraving and Printing, produces the nation's dollar and coin supply.

_____ The 12 Federal Reserve Banks are nationwide, and each serves a specific region of the country; along with the Board of Governors in Washington, D.C.

_____ All monopolies are bad.

_____ The Fed was started in 1933.

103/128

Name _____
Date _____
Score _____

Fill in the blanks (each answer, 2 points).

1. 1929 was the year in which the Stock Market crash started the Great _____ .

2. In a 52 weeks high and low, if the numbers show _____ difference between each other, there is less risk of loss - but there is also less opportunity for gain, either.

3. Look closely at the volume number—if a tiny "z" is shown before the number, the volume is not given in hundreds but is the _____ of stocks traded.

4. A price-earnings ratio is figured out by calculating the relationship between the price of the company's stock and the _____ a company makes in the entire _____ . It is figured out by dividing the closing price of a stock by the earnings per share of each stock.

5. When you told the broker you wanted to get those six shares of Mattel® stock, he sent a message to a person who is working on the _____ of the New York Stock Exchange®.

6. The very first stock exchange was created in 1531 in Antwerp, _____ .

7. After the _____ , Wall Street became more important and the New York Stock Exchange® was getting all the business it could handle.

8. In the 1700s the first banks in American history were being created and _____ was needed to make the start successful.

9. Jim receives a copy of a new radio station being proposed in his town. Within the information he learns the potential for profits, the risk involved and how much capital is needed in order to become a shareholder. Jim is looking at a _____ .

10. In our story, the broker tells you, "Well, right now a share in Mattel® Toys is going for 10 dollars (not the actual price), but my _____ will cost you 40 dollars, so you can buy six shares of Mattel®."

11. A broker is the person who will do the actual _____ of the stocks for you.

12. When you call a broker and arrange to buy stock, the broker calls a person on the floor of the exchange, probably an _____ of his.

13. Give the two examples provided that represent a blue chip stock: _____ and _____ .

14. A share of profits received by a shareholder is called a _____ .

15. _____ are the safest stock investment you can make, since these corporations are so large and powerful they can withstand a downturn in the economy.

16. After all expenses are subtracted, the amount of money left after a sale is called a _____ .

17. Selling directly to the consumer with costs included to cover manufacturing, advertising, overhead and other concerns is called _____ .

18. A question to ask yourself before you invest any money is: How has the company been doing against its _____ ?

19. Whenever you buy stock, you will then be referred to as a shareholder or _____ .

20. If you don't see a demand for a product, it's best to be _____ buying stock from that company.

21. Whenever you enter the business world of purchasing stocks, you must realize that this is not _____ .

22. The record-breaking, dead-bottom low of the stock market crash did not come until July, 1932, as the market had lost approximately _____ % of its value.

23. Percentage-wise, the 1987 stock market crash was _____ than the 1929 crash.

Matching (each answer, 2 points).

24. _____ volatility
25. _____ volume

26. _____ penny stocks

27. _____ high, low and close
28. _____ common stock
29. _____ downturn
30. _____ dividend

31. _____ issue

a. a dip in the market

b. the activity of a stock; the highest price and lowest price of the stock, along with the closing price on a given day

c. the risk and profit potential of a particular stock

d. number of stocks traded in a day

e. the act of a company selling stock

f. a share of profits received by a shareholder

g. most basic stock a company will issue; it carries higher risks than other stocks

h. considered the first and lowest level of stocks; usually going to stay small

Matching (each answer, 2 points).

32. _____ dip

33. _____ share

34. _____ stock exchange

35. _____ stock certificate

36. _____ American Stock Exchange®

37. _____ New York Stock Exchange®

38. _____ broker services

39. _____ discount brokerage

a. the largest of all American stock exchanges, created in 1792

b. work done or the shareholder by the broker, such as selling and buying stock

c. offers significant discounts for conducting purchases over the Internet

d. a unit of the equal parts of the capital stock divided by a corporation

e. the formal name of the curb traders; it began in 1908

f. a place where financial securities are bought and sold

g. a form of proof of possession of stock; mostly obsolete nowadays

h. a drop in the market which may signify a good time to buy stocks

Matching (each answer, 2 points).

40. _____ crash

    a. one who believes the outlook for a market or stock is up

41. _____ demand

    b. a standard unit of value in the stock market

42. _____ climb

    c. similar to a rise in the market and signifies a good time to buy if you are looking to purchase stocks

43. _____ bear

    d. a call for a product or service; a need or want

44. _____ point

    e. October 19, 1987

45. _____ bull

    f. one who believes the outlook for a market or stock is down

True/False (each answer, 2 points).

46. _____ The activity the day before; the highest price and lowest price of the stock, along with the closing price at the end of the business day will be noted on the stock page as "high, low and close."

47. _____ The stock market in America started in the 1800s.

48. _____ From its humble origins the New York Stock Exchange® has grown to be a financial force in the world today.

49. _____ Symbols are usually one, two or three letters.

50. _____ A preferred stock is a financial return that has a set limit.

51. _____ When you buy stocks, you are buying a small percentage of everything owned by the company. This includes computers, desks and bookshelves, among other things.

The floor broker purchases your six shares of Mattel® and then reports the trade to the floor. That means that hundreds of computers all over the NYSE have recorded your (2 points)

52. _____ transaction.

    _____ unemployment.

    _____ PIN number.

    _____ embezzlements.

Which statement(s) is/are TRUE? (2 points)

53. _____ The Wall Street Journal® is the daily newspaper which focuses on stock market activity.

    _____ A transaction is written proof that a purchase has been made.

    _____ If you want to buy shares in Mattel® Toys, you run down to Toys R Us® and tell them you want twenty shares of Mattel®

    _____ AMEX® is another name for the Standard & Poor® index.

    _____ A counselor is the person who will do the actual purchasing of the stocks for you.

    _____ When you purchase a share, you have purchased a little piece of the prospectus.

    _____ People will subscribe to publications such as Barron's® or The Wall Street Journal® to get information on investing more wisely.

    _____ Mattel®, as well as thousands of other companies, offers the opportunity to buy a part of their company by selling shares.

Which of these words is NOT a name for a stock? (2 points)

54.   _____   equities

        _____   tickers

        _____   securities

        _____   issues

        _____   shares

Which statements are TRUE   (each answer, 2 points).

55.   _____   The Standard & Poor® list contains the 500 largest publicly held companies.

        _____   Your portfolio is all of the various stocks or bonds your broker cannot allow you to purchase.

        _____   First, all the common stock in a company must be issued. Then the company will begin to issue preferred stock.

        _____   Your portfolio is all of the various stocks or bonds you, as an investor, hold.

        _____   Standard & Poor's® 500 is a type of stock index favored by professionals because it includes a far smaller range of public companies than the Dow Jones℠ industrial average does.

        _____   If the company has been making a good profit against competition, you may continue to see that profit grow and that is a good sign for investing.

        _____   If you don't see any profit from the company recently, that's a sign it may be a good business for investment.

        _____   Putting money into stocks is a risky thing.

Which of these two statements is TRUE? (2 points)

56.   _____   In reality, both the 1929 and the 1987 crashes were started by people who had one thing in mind: embezzlement.

        _____   When the market is trying to steady itself out after a monumental movement, it is called a correction.

112/140

Name _____
Date _____
Score _____

Complete the following questions (each answer, 2 points).

1. PIN stands for _____ .

2. _____ is the job of putting loan applications into official consideration.

3. "Not for _____ , not for charity, but for _____" is a credit union motto.

4. As soon as all members in early SLA associations received their loans and started on _____ payments to pay back the loans, the association pretty much started closing down. It was almost like a club of would-be _____ buyers.

5. _____ are checks which function almost like cash but are replaceable if lost or stolen.

6. The place where you bought the travelers checks is called the _____ bank or agency.

7. Before a trip, find a well-known company that charges no fees and that have checks that almost any business would recognize. American Express® and _____ offer travelers checks for no fee.

8. Many employers offer direct deposit of _____ to a credit union.

9. Proverbs:13:11—"Wealth [gotten] by vanity shall be diminished: but he that gathereth by labour shall _____ ." In other words a person who tries to get money by fraudulent means will not get more, but the steady worker will add to his _____ .

10. Proverbs 23:4-5—"Labour not to be _____ : cease from thine own wisdom. Wilt thou set thine eyes upon that which is not?"

11. When you have listed all your income and expenses and want to find out how much you have left over, subtract the _____ from _____ and see what comes out on the "bottom line."

12. Official permission to postpone the payments of a loan is known as a _____ .

13. _____ is a percentage of the amount loaned which is a charge for the use of the money.

14. It is important to pay back your student loan. Besides your Christian testimony being damaged, other problems could arise. The default could be reported to national _____ and a negative history will stay on your report.

15. The amount of spending that the credit card company will allow you is known as the _____ .

16. An _____ card often donates part of its fee to the sponsoring organization.

Match each word with its correct meaning (each answer, 2 points).

17. _____ field of membership

18. _____ ATM

19. _____ credit history

20. _____ serial number

a. the fee will show up on your next monthly statement

b. a percentage of the amount in the savings account which is a reward for the bank's use of the money

c. accounted for 59 percent of all home loans in 1987

d. stretching one's credit beyond the financial guidelines

21. _____ time deposit
22. _____ annual return
23. _____ overextending
24. _____ SLA's
25. _____ interest
26. _____ If you withdrawal from a "foreign" ATM

e. a deposit that gives a certain amount of interest in a specified amount of time

f. the amount a savings account will earn on interest in the course of a calendar year

g. specific number for the purpose of verification and location in case of theft or misplacement

h. a years-long record of how well a person pays their bills and is financially responsible

i. can allow withdrawals up to $200 or $300 a day

j. the range of eligibility for a credit union, such as a teacher's credit union or a bricklayer's credit union

Answer *true* **or false** (each answer, 2 points).

27. _____ Monthly statements are a regularly mailed account of your bank transactions and financial activity.

28. _____ All states in the U.S. have rules to set limits on how much an ATM surcharge can be.

29. _____ When we talk about a "ceiling" on the interest rate, we are referring to the limit on the interest given.

30. _____ Certificates of deposit show the penalties you incur when you deposit too much in one business day.

31. _____ There was once a time when banks were not allowed to merge or even expand outside their county.

32. _____ Credit unions serve groups of people that share something common, such as where they work or live.

33. _____ Oxford Provident was such a success that a new form of SLA was created–the serial association.

34. _____ If you just want to cash your travelers check instead of purchasing something, you need to remember that there may be a fee.

35. _____ A debit card is a card that acts like a check. When you make a purchase, the money is removed from your checking account immediately.

36. _____ Each travelers check has a Social Security number to help identify it in case it is stolen.

37. _____ It is easy to tell yourself "it's only ten dollars," but you will find yourself saying that again and again until you wonder where your money has gone.

38. _____ Some banks offer interest on the money that is in the checking account.

39. _____ Never charge more on your credit cards than you can afford to pay in one month.

40. _____ A loan that will charge you interest from the start is called an unsubsidized loan.

41. _____ Under the Fair Credit and Charge Card Disclosure Act, you have the right to comparison shop different cards' terms and conditions.

42. _____ The great thing about IRAs is that you can withdraw money anytime you want with no financial penalty.

43. _____ Remember to take the car for a spin and let your mechanic friend feel how the car responds to accelerating up hills.

44. _____ Card issuers are not allowed to charge a fee when you use the card to obtain a cash advance.

Match each word with its correct meaning (each answer, 2 points).

45. _____ FFEL Stafford Loan   a. also called a "grace period"

46. _____ processed   b. a guarantee that is legally binding to hold the dealership to what it has promised

47. _____ warranty   c. assistance from the government which is not to be repaid

48. _____ free period   d. assistance from the government which is to be repaid

49. _____ Federal Pell Grant   e. actions which take the check from the merchant to the accounting centers of the bank; the steps that will carry the check through its full payment

Choose the correct answer for the following questions (each answer, 2 points).

50. Charges that your bank must pay if you use an ATM that is "foreign," meaning not owned by your bank are called _____ .

    a. withdrawal penalties   b. interchange fees

51. When you use _____ , your paycheck is electronically transferred into the depositors account without the depositor having to come to the physical location of the credit union office.

    a. sponsor   b. field of membership   c. state charter   d. direct deposit

52. A consumer can buy products in bulk at a _____ .

    a. bank branch   b. warehouse club   c. barter exchange

Mark the statements which are NOT true? (each answer, 2 points)

53. a. ____ A password is a coded word or number used to provide security to the cardholder. It is a security measure offered by the bank.

    b. ____ Surcharges are added fees for various services, so it is best to make sure what charges you incur when you use an ATM.

    c. ____ If Wild Westbank, the ATM owner, levies a $1.50 surcharge, then your $20 withdrawal will appear on your receipt as $21.50, even though all you received was $18.50.

    d. ____ The program to access to find out about your personal account balances is called an inquiry.

    e. ____ Banks normally levy ATM surcharges only on customers of other banks.

54. a. ____ A "rollover" IRA is one that gets money from another foreign business.

    b. ____ An affinity card issuer donates a portion of the annual fees or transaction charges to the sponsoring organization.

    c. ____ Keep your credit card receipts and promptly compare them when your bills arrive.

55. a. ____ A serial association was the second form of a savings and loan, where the end result was to find new ways of financial assistance rather than closing down after a project was completed.

    b. ____ Annual means once a year.

    c. ____ One of the equal parts divided up by a corporation is called a share.

    d. ____ Oxford Provident Building Association was the first SLA in America, created in 1831 in Frankfort, Pennsylvania.

    e. ____ Semiannual means once every two years.

56.   a. ____   Nehemiah 10:37 is one of the Bible passages concerning the tithing principle.

      b. ____   A bookstore is a good alternative to a library.

      c. ____   An explanation of how the card's balances are determined is required to appear on billing statements.

      d. ____   Proverbs 23:4-5 warns us against an unhealthy desire for wealth.

      e. ____   Biblical tithing basically means you will give 10 percent of your income to the Lord.

Mark the statements which are TRUE (each answer, 2 points).

57.   a. ____   There are more than 102,000 federal-chartered and state-chartered credit unions nationwide.

      b. ____   The first credit union in the United States was formed in Manchester, New Hampshire, in 1909.

      c. ____   Credit unions exist for one year, then shut down after everyone pays off their loan.

      d. ____   The National Credit Union Share Insurance Fund is an agency for the federal government and insures deposits of credit union members up to $1,000.

58.   a. ____   A contribution is a financial cooperative that provides loans to its members at lower rates of interest than would be available at other institutions.

      b. ____   A "cooperative" is another name for a loan.

      c. ____   SLAs pay earnings in regular installments to their members, but continue to finance homes and charge interest.

      d. ____   You cannot take out a car loan from your Savings and Loan Association.

59.   a. ____   Making a purchase on the spur of the moment and without careful planning is called stewardship.

      b. ____   Proverbs 21:20 tells us, "[There is] treasure…and oil in the dwelling of the wise, but a foolish man spendeth it up." The writer is telling us that the wise man will save what he can.

      c. ____   Factory direct is manufacturer-to-consumer selling.

      d. ____   Frivolous means trendy and up-to-date.

60.   a. ____   If you are trying to keep a budget, checking accounts are a better system of accountability than cash.

      b. ____   In some cases banks have charged anywhere from $18 to $25 for an overdraft.

      c. ____   It is okay to overlook a "small" expense. It is not that much of your overall budget.

      d. ____   When you talk with a customer service representative, you can tell them of your particular needs in opening a checking account.

      e. ____   One of the steps towards what people call a "cashless society" was when the postal currency was introduced.

61.   a. ____   The Expected Family Contribution is the assumed amount that the family will contribute to the student's college tuition and other expenses.

      b. ____   A default is a failure to fulfill a financial position.

      c. ____   A credit bureau reports the college's financial position.

      d. ____   A loan that will charge you a contribution is called an unsubsidized loan.

History & Geography 1210 Alternate Test

Name _____

Date _____

Score _____

Fill in the blanks (each answer 3 points).

1. The Statue of Liberty was a gift from _____ to the United States in 1876.

2. Concerns with wild fluctuations in the worth of their country's money led some _____ nations to join in the effort for a unified unit of currency.

3. This red, white and blue stripped flag is the flag of _____.

4. This green and red flag is the flag of _____.

5. The world's largest auto trade show occurs each year in _____.

6. _____ has the largest economy of any EU nation.

7. The United States Census Bureau reports that, among religions, _____ make up more than 50% of the population.

8. American Samoa is one of the United States' _____.

9. The state that touches the northern border of Texas is _____.

10. _____ are extended, narrow arms of the sea that are bordered by majestic high, rocky cliffs.

11. Two-thirds of Japan is covered in mountains and sprinkled with more than _____ volcanoes.

12. One of the main towns to visit in Norway is Bodo, especially during the June to July months. This town experiences the midnight _____ during that spell - there is virtually no nighttime during that period!

13. Israeli Prime Minister Yitzak Rabin was assassinated by _____.

14. A meditation room with a Buddhist-type appearance is called a _____.

15. One who, by dying, gives witness to his faith is called a _____.

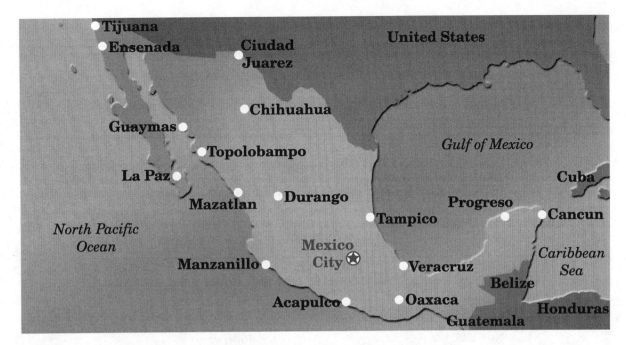

Study the map, then answer the questions below (each answer, 3 points).

16.   The city of Mazatlan is located along the _____ .

       The city of Ciudad Juarez is located _____ .

       The body of water east of Mexico is _____ .

17.   A look at the map of Mexico shows us that Guatemala and _____
       share Mexico's southern border.

Matching (each answer, 2 points).

18. _____ Spain   a. a boot-shaped country

19. _____ Italy   b. over 82% of the population of this country is
                                      Lutheran

20. _____ Slovakia   c. the capital city of this country is Madrid

21. _____ Finland   d. the name of London's airport

22. _____ Belgium   e. this country is home to the European
                                      Commission

23. _____ Heathrow   f. the capital city of this country is Bratislava

24. _____ Ahnighito   g. the name of London's public transportation
                                      system

25. _____ Underground   h. the largest meteorite retrieved from Earth's
                                      surface

Matching (each answer, 2 points).

26. _____ Victoria   a. headquarters of the United Nations

27. _____ London   b. capital city of Canada

28. _____ Zurich   c. an area twice the size of Washington D.C

29. _____ New York   d. a financial center located in Australia

30. _____ Los Angeles   e. second largest city in the United States

31. _____ Toronto   f. a city in the Swiss Alps

32. _____ Sydney   g. ¼ of the world's financial companies have headquarters in this city

33. _____ Gaza Strip   h. the capital city of Hong Kong

Match the state with its capital (each answer, 2 points).

34. _____ North Dakota   a. Montpelier

35. _____ Arizona   b. Richmond

36. _____ Virginia   c. Madison

37. _____ Colorado   d. Phoenix

38. _____ New York   e. Little Rock

39. _____ Wisconsin   f. Denver

40. _____ Vermont   g. Trenton

41. _____ New Mexico   h. Santa Fe

42. _____ Arkansas   i. Albany

43. _____ New Jersey   j. Bismarck

Matching (each answer, 2 points).

44. _____ Matthew Perry   a. four major islands (Hokkaido, Honshu, Shikoku and Kyushu) and thousands of smaller ones

45. _____ Prince Edward Island   b. opened trade with Japan in 1853

46. _____ Japan   c. a maritime province; Charlottetown is the capital city

Matching (each answer, 2 points).

47. _____ Nova Scotia   a. Regina is the capital city

48. _____ Saskatchewan   b. a maritime province; Halifax is the capital city

49. _____ New Brunswick   c. a maritime province; Fredericton is the capital city

Matching (each answer, 2 points).

50. _____ Gaza Strip

51. _____ Northwest Territories

52. _____ 750,000 Jews

a. Yellowknife is the capital city

b. entered Israel from the U.S.S.R. in the early 1990s

c. located along the Mediterranean Sea

True/False (each answer 2 points).

53. _____ Ireland has a coastline that touches the North Atlantic Ocean.

54. _____ The national capital of Belgium is Amsterdam.

55. _____ Hong Kong was once a British colony.

56. _____ The state of Washington is located just to the south of Oregon.

57. _____ Mexico City has a population of more than 40 million people.

58. _____ Prussia was declared defunct by the Axis powers at the conclusion of World War II.

59. _____ Israel is slightly smaller than the state of California.

Which western Canadian province shares a border with the state of Washington? (2 points)

60. _____ Alberta

_____ British Columbia

_____ Saskatchewan

_____ Quebec

_____ Ontario

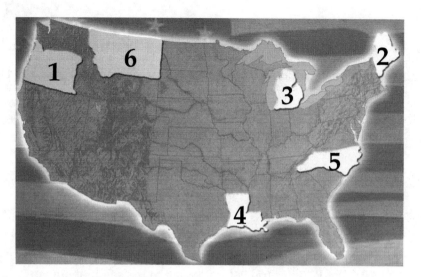

Name the numbered states and their capital city (each answer, 3 points).

61.   State 1: _____ Capital city: _____

        State 2: _____ Capital city: _____

        State 3: _____ Capital city: _____

        State 4: _____ Capital city: _____

        State 5: _____ Capital city: _____

        State 6: _____ Capital city: _____

ANSWER KEYS

SECTION ONE

1.1 they enforce rules that control conduct within a population.

1.2 local, state, federal

1.3
- Local governments help the citizen by creating libraries, such as in the town of Delmar, Delaware.
- Public utilities include telephone and electricity supplied to the citizen.
- Towns can create and maintain local parks.
- The state government has the right to make and enforce laws within their home.

1.4 false

1.5 Federal

1.6 purchase, trade, sale

1.7 gas, telephone, electric power, water

1.8 c

1.9 b

1.10 a

1.11 e

1.12 d

1.13 Exodus

1.14 (answers will vary): mass transportation, mass transit, libraries, local parks, town streets

1.15 Aristotle

1.16 true

1.17 f

1.18 d

1.19 c

1.20 e

1.21 a

1.22 b

1.23 totalitarianism

1.24 pluralism

1.25 anarchism

1.26 racial, ethnic, business

1.27 jurisdiction

1.28 Morality

1.29 dictator

1.30 [Idi] Amin

1.31 bureaucracy

1.32 Habeas Corpus

1.33 autocracy

1.34 foreign exchange

1.35 welfare state

1.36 an autocracy

SECTION TWO

2.1 four

2.2 veto

2.3 the Senate, House of Representatives

2.4 life

2.5 Constitution

2.6 two thirds

2.7 high officials or Supreme Court members

2.8 Romans

2.9 Supreme Court justices

2.10 parliamentary

2.11 life peers

2.12 "House of Commons," "House of Lords"

2.13 Prime Minister

2.14 abdications

2.15 six

2.16 democratic

2.17 they are both appointed for life

2.18 a

2.19 d

2.20 b

2.21 e

2.22 c

2.23 true

2.24 false

2.25 false

2.26 dictatorships

2.27 Communist

2.28 six

2.29-2.33 (answers will vary): Japan, France, Belgium, Italy, Denmark, Sri Lanka

2.34 PRI, 70

2.35 liberal, moderate, conservative

2.36 1 Timothy

2.37 salvation

2.38 atrocity

2.39 e

2.40 b

2.41 d

2.42 c

2.43 a

2.44
- It is considered a democracy with a one party system
- It actually has several small but ineffective political parties,
- The Institutional Revolutionary Party has been in control since the 1920s.

2.45 Mexico

2.46 recruits members and leaders.
develops policy.
indoctrinates the people.
maintains discipline.

SECTION THREE

3.1 revolutionary

3.2 culture

3.3 oppressive

3.4 theology

3.5 384 B.C.

3.6 true

3.7 Summa Theologica

3.8 •assisting in the early education of Alexander the Great.

•writing Nechomachean Ethics.

3.9 Great personal fulfillment is achieved when a person is given the freedom to pursue his dreams.

3.10 Engels edited Marx's The Condition of the Working Class in England.

3.11 It allows the citizen to own and operate private business for profit.

3.12 a

3.13 d

3.14 b

3.15 e

3.16 c

3.17 *Of Reformation in England*
The Ready and Easy Way to Establish a Commonwealth
The Tenure of Kings and Magistrates

3.18 Niccolo Machiavelli

3.19 dissenter

3.20 Das Kapital

3.21 1600s, monarchy

3.22 Judges 2:19

3.23 monarch

3.24 It approved of the use of force upon dissenters.
It approved cruelty and deceitfulness to maintain the balance of power.

SECTION ONE

1.1 d

1.2 b

1.3 a

1.4 c

1.5 e

1.6 Congress may not establish a religion and Congress may not keep a religion from free exercise.

1.7 Bill of Rights

1.8 taxes, enforcing

1.9 peacefulness, calmness

1.10 criminal, state

1.11 persecute

1.12 assemble

1.13 correcting a wrong that was done.

1.14 39, 1787

1.15 a prayer requirement in public schools.

1.16 •It lays out the general method for electing a president.
•It deals with establishing copyrights for inventors.

1.17 false

1.18 true

1.19 No excessive bail; no excessive punishment is allowed.

1.20 George Mason

1.21 immunities, freedoms

1.22 disobeyed or violated

1.23 trial

1.24 list

1.25 listed, right

1.26 states, people

1.27 12

1.28 keep and bear arms

1.29 •Soldiers may not be improperly quartered in a citizen's home.
•School shall not be mandatory for children under the age of fifteen.

1.30 e

1.31 f

1.32 a

1.33 c

1.34 d

1.35 b

1.36 state bar exam

1.37 Jurisdiction

1.38 treaties

1.39 public works

1.40 10

1.41 The state of Pennsylvania oversees the inner workings of the Electoral College.

1.42 A hospital would be included in the public safety service.

1.43 marriages, dental practices, auto registration, real estate brokers, lawyers.

SECTION TWO

2.1   e

2.2   a

2.3   c

2.4   f

2.5   b

2.6   d

2.7   interpret

2.8   executive, legislative, judicial

2.9   diplomatic relations

2.10   2

2.11   false

2.12   true

2.13   false

2.14   The "Beltway mentality" is a desired goal of every presidential administration.

2.15   •National Security Council.
•Office of Policy Development.
•Office of Management and Budget.
•Council of Economic Advisors.
•White House office.

2.16   e

2.17   d

2.18   a

2.19   c

2.20   f

2.21   b

2.22   either: negate, destroy

2.23   nominates

2.24   Article III

2.25   either: nominated, chosen, approved.

2.26   Statutory construction

2.27   Constitution, violation, nullify

2.28   judiciary branch of the government.

2.29   •The judiciary system is established by the Constitution.
•Nine justices serve in the Supreme Court.
•There are 12 courts of appeal in the judiciary system.

2.30   The impeachment process of a federal judge only comes through the president's approval.

2.31   d

2.32   f

2.33   a

2.34   b

2.35   c

2.36   e

2.37   divided government

2.38   ambassador

2.39   Article I

2.40   100, 435

2.41   most recent U.S. Census

2.42   repeal

2.43   •General Accounting Office
•Government Printing Office
•Library of Congress
•Congressional Budget Office

2.44   true

2.45   true

2.46   president pro tempore

SECTION THREE

3.1	d	3.16	f
3.2	e	3.17	c
3.3	b	3.18	b
3.4	a	3.19	d
3.5	c	3.20	e
3.6	voted it down	3.21	a
3.7	changes, amendments	3.22	A chamber is a legislative meeting hall.
3.8	draft		
3.9	the subcommittee lets it set and does nothing	3.23	true
		3.24	true
3.10	House	3.25	false
3.11	false	3.26	true
3.12	true	3.27	concurrence
3.13	false	3.28	versions
3.14	Ordering a bill reported: A subcommittee reads its recommendation to both houses of Congress.		
3.15	H.R. signifies a House bill and S. a Senate bill.		

SECTION ONE

1.1	b
1.2	c
1.3	f
1.4	a
1.5	e
1.6	d
1.7	instruments
1.8	Democratic, Republican
1.9	Canada, Great Britain, US
1.10	Labor, Conservative
1.11	partisans
1.12	The voters in a district who elect a public servant.
1.13	(answers may vary): Communist, Fascist, One Party
1.14	(answers may vary): Jackson, Van Buren, Polk, Pierce, Buchanan, Cleveland, Wilson, Tyler, Roosevelt, Truman, Kennedy, Johnson, Carter, Clinton.
1.15	partisan politics
1.16	Thomas Jefferson
1.17	strengthening the two major parties
1.18	Democrat
1.19	a temporary alliance of political parties.
1.20	Democrat
1.21	true
1.22	false
1.23	loose construction
1.24	federal government
1.25	strict construction
1.26	1840 and 1848
1.27	Breckinridge, Douglas
1.28	Grover Cleveland, Woodrow Wilson

1.29	(answers may vary): Lincoln, Grant, Hayes, Harrison, Mckinley, Ford, Johnson, Garfield, Hoover, Arthur, Roosevelt, Taft, Harding, Coolidge, Eisenhower, Nixon, Reagan, Bush
1.30	a
1.31	c
1.32	b
1.33	d
1.34	d
1.35	b
1.36	c
1.37	a
1.38	e
1.39	f
1.40	the powers the constitution delegated to it
1.41	• It is the oldest political party in the US. • The Democrats won the presidency in the 90s but lost control of the Congress.
1.42	all of the above
1.43	true
1.44	c
1.45	d
1.46	b
1.47	a
1.48	true
1.49	false
1.50	true
1.51	true
1.52	true
1.53	true
1.54	true

SECTION ONE (cont.)

1.55   true

1.56   false

1.57   false

1.58   false

1.59   ownership

1.60   (answers will vary): Progressive
        Party, Bull Moose Party, Dixiecrats
        Party, American Independent Party,
        Liberal Republicans Party, Gold
        Democrats Party, Greenback Party,
        Prohibition Party, American

Communist Party, New Party,
Natural Law Party, United We Stand
Party, Reform Party, Libertarian
Party, The Green Party, The US
Taxpayers Party, Communist Party
U.S.A.

1.61   incumbent

1.62   a party that has only one goal

1.63   American Communist Party

1.64   specific group of people

SECTION TWO

2.1 d

2.2 e

2.3 f

2.4 a

2.5 b

2.6 c

2.7 Persian Gulf, economy

2.8 Planks are parts of the party platform in the form of issues that are presented to the people. For example: civil rights, taxes and energy.

2.9 They can be involved by marking a box on his/her tax return requesting that a certain amount of his tax go into the presidential campaign fund.

2.10 loyal opposition

2.11 (private) donations

2.12 all of the above

2.13 every 4 years

2.14 national committee

2.15 9.6 million dollars

2.16 f

2.17 e

2.18 a

2.19 b

2.20 c

2.21 d

2.22 the Party candidate for president

2.23 Washington D.C.

2.24 *The Republican, The Democrat Digest*

2.25 Party Primaries, Convention

2.26 captain, committeeman

2.27 honesty

2.28 mass meeting, committee

2.29 •if most members in the Congress from his states are Republican.
•if his state has a Republican governor.
•his state cast electoral votes in the last election for the Republican candidate.

2.30 all of the above

2.31 true

2.32 c

2.33 b

2.34 a

2.35 true

2.36 true

2.37 to talk

2.38 nomination

2.39 electoral college

2.40 caucus

2.41 local

2.42 delegates

2.43 people, party leaders

2.44 county, state

2.45 officers, chairmen, delegates

2.46 officers, Congress, delegates

SECTION TWO (cont.)

2.47 It allows them to take care of other party business besides nominating candidates of the party they desire.

2.48 fraud, bribery, corruption

2.49 declaration and payment

2.50 open, closed

2.51 An open primary is on in which voters may vote for the candidates of the party they desire.

2.52 A closed primary is a nominating election in which each voter gets the ballot of his/her announced party.

2.53 (answers will vary): Wisconsin, Idaho, Montana

2.54 The voter is given one ballot that has the names of the candidates for each office in each party. The voter makes his choice regardless of the party label of the candidate for whom he votes.

2.55 petition, self announcement

2.56 primary

2.57 officers, filing fee

2.58 independent

2.59 caucus, convention, direct primary petition, announcement

2.60 states

SECTION THREE

3.1   f

3.2   b

3.3   a

3.4   d

3.5   e

3.6   c

3.7   The voters cannot possibly learn enough about the candidates for all offices to vote intelligently.

3.8   straight ticket

3.9   split ticket

3.10 candidate

3.11 short

3.12 four

3.13 unopposed

3.14 true

3.15 false

3.16 true

3.17 false

3.18 false

3.19 true

3.20 true

3.21 true

3.22 e

3.23 a

3.24 b

3.25 f

3.26 d

3.27 c

3.28 precincts

3.29 400

3.30 schools, police stations, fire stations, libraries

3.31 three, five

3.32 county supervisors, district election board

3.33 orally

3.34 Australian

3.35 Louisville, Kentucky

3.36 it is a secret ballot, names of all candidates appear on a single ballot, it is prepared by the state or county at public expense, distributed at polling places by election officials.

3.37 recount

3.38 Once you have reached the proper age you will need to register. You will receive a card that tells you where to go to vote in your precinct. On election day you go to the poll, give your name and address, and after everything checks out you are given a ballot. You then go to the booth, mark your ballot in secret and fold it. You then hand the ballot to the election officer who puts it in the ballot box.

3.39 business, ill/sick, disabled

3.40 mail

3.41 notary public, clerk

3.42 true

3.43 election board

3.44 all of the above

SECTION ONE

1.1   c

1.2   colony

1.3   socialist

1.4   Sam Houston

1.5   Production, sustenance

1.6   Pittsburgh

1.7   Diotrephes

1.8   b

1.9   d

1.10 c

1.11 a

1.12 e

1.13 •The government should have a goal

      •Safety is a priority

      •Leadership is needed

      •Law and order should be maintained

      •Production and sustenance should be provided daily

1.14 b

1.15 d

1.16 f

1.17 e

1.18 a

1.19 c

1.20 Solon established a law which enslaved people in debt.

1.21 city-states

1.22 Cleisthenes

1.23 750 B.C.

1.24 594

1.25 d

1.26 c

1.27 e

1.28 a

1.29 b

1.30 true

1.31 false

1.32 false

1.33 true

1.34 [the] Concilum Plebus

1.35 27

1.36 patrician

1.37 empire

1.38 450 B.C.

1.39 The Romans' first code of law was established around 450 B.C.

1.40 c

1.41 e

1.42 f

1.43 a

1.44 d

1.45 b

1.46 Samnites, Celtics, Etruscans, Carthaginians

1.47 •In Rome, only men with money and property could vote.

      •In Greece all men were allowed to vote.

      •In the Roman Senate, the most powerful part of the government, all senators were patricians

1.48 true

1.49 false

SECTION TWO

2.1	c	2.25	false
2.2	d	2.26	Judges
2.3	e	2.27	my son
2.4	f	2.28	Exodus
2.5	a	2.29	death
2.6	b	2.30	c
2.7	protection	2.31	a
2.8	homage	2.32	b
2.9	subinfeudation	2.33	e
2.10	b	2.34	f
2.11	b	2.35	c
2.12	a, c	2.36	a
2.13	c	2.37	b
2.14	c	2.38	d
2.15	d	2.39	1996
2.16	e	2.40	direct democracy
2.17	a	2.41	representatives, district
2.18	b	2.42	1991
2.19	true	2.43	true

2.20 We still carry the idea of one presiding authority, a judge, and peers who will help in the decision making process, a jury. A vassal would answer a summons.

2.21 First Samuel, chapter 12 tells of the prophet Samuel's displeasure over the nation's desire for monarchy.

2.22	true	2.44	false
2.23	false	2.45	d
2.24	true		

2.46 •opportunity for education
•equality before the law
•the citizen's freedom
•voting rights

2.47	b
2.48	d
2.49	e
2.50	a
2.51	c

SECTION THREE

3.1 e

3.2 f

3.3 d

3.4 c

3.5 a

3.6 b

3.7 "Might makes right" or "Ruling by Strength"

3.8 World War II

3.9 rods, axe

3.10 freedom of worship
cultural pursuits

3.11 Fascists usually gain power after a country's economic collapse.

3.12 •The Axis powers were a coalition of countries that opposed the Allied powers in World War II.
•Political, economic, social and even religious activities are under the rule of a fascist government.
•A fascist government is usually controlled by a dictator.

3.13 b

3.14 a

3.15 c

3.16 f

3.17 d

3.18 e

3.19 a

3.20 b

3.21 h

3.22 i

3.23 j

3.24 g

3.25 false

3.26 true

3.27 false

3.28 true

3.29 true

3.30 William Penn

3.31 concentration camps

SECTION ONE

1.1   a. g   e. g
      b. g   f. g
      c. b   g. b
      d. b   h. b

1.2   c

1.3   e

1.4   f

1.5   b

1.6   a

1.7   d

1.8   c

1.9   e

1.10   d

1.11   a

1.12   b

1.13   I will do

1.14   neutrality

1.15   American Civil Liberties Union

1.16   multi-cultural

1.17   true

1.18   true

1.19   false

1.20   a. the government is forbidden to establish religion.
      b. the government is forbidden to interfere with or regulate religion.

1.21   d

1.22   c

1.23   e

1.24   f

1.25   a

1.26   b

1.27   Slavery was an established institution until the Twelfth Amendment was ratified on December 18, 1865.

1.28   Romans 10:12

1.29   segregation

1.30   fathers, nation

1.31   social rewards

1.32   e

1.33   b

1.34   a

1.35   b

1.36   a

1.37   c

1.38   a

1.39   It was a nonviolent demonstration in the form of civil rights rally held in Washington, D.C. on August 28, 1963. Some 200,000 people (African American and White), who supported the cause of equal rights, peacefully illustrated their impatience with slow government action concerning civil rights. A key speaker for the rally was Dr. Martin Luther King.

1.40   true

1.41   true

1.42   true

1.43   false

1.44   false

1.45   c

1.46   a

1.47   d

1.48   b

1.49   e

1.50   h

1.51   j

1.52   g

1.53   k

1.54   f

1.55   l

1.56   i

SECTION ONE (cont.)

1.57   true

1.58   false

1.59   true

1.60   France, Jews

1.61   the Great Melting Pot

1.62   Onesimus

1.63   freedom

1.64   wealthy, poor

1.65   love

1.66   each is to esteem others higher than themselves.

SECTION TWO

2.1   d

2.2   e

2.3   b

2.4   a

2.5   c

2.6   particular issue

2.7   voice

2.8   experts

2.9   mutual concession

2.10   facts

2.11   pressure groups

2.12   pamphlets, books,
       articles, newspaper columns

2.13   false

2.14   Determine how people will vote in
       elections and determine the
       popularity of the individual as well
       as government policies.

2.15   Gallup Poll, Harris Poll

2.16   government

2.17   opinions

2.18   b

2.19   c

2.20   a

2.21   e

2.22   d

2.23   g

2.24   f

2.25   (answers may vary)
       newspaper, magazines, television,
       radio, motion pictures, friends,
       family, church, internet

2.26   editors

2.27   advertisers

2.28   Matthew 24:4

2.29   News and World Report

2.30   audio, visual

2.31   editors

2.32   "Meet the Press," "Face the Nation"

2.33   reform(s)

2.34   education

2.35   true

2.36   false

2.37   d

2.38   Because it is impossible to tell the
       whole truth in only a few seconds.

2.39   On the radio you can only hear the
       speaker. On the television you can see
       the speaker, observe his movements
       and gestures, all the little tricks of
       public speaking.

SECTION THREE

3.1   c

3.2   d

3.3   h

3.4   e

3.5   a

3.6   b

3.7   f

3.8   g

3.9   David, Moses, Solomon

3.10 Treasury

3.11 Boy's State, Girl's State

3.12 Judas

3.13 (answers will vary)
civics, government, history, economics, sociology, problems of democracy

3.14 Jackson Day, Lincoln Day

3.15 To get to know the inner workings and purpose of political parties and to get qualified people to serve in government.

3.16 b

3.17 e

3.18 c

3.19 f

3.20 a

3.21 d

3.22 i

3.23 j

3.24 g

3.25 h

3.26 plain folks

3.27 glittering generalities

3.28 5:9

3.29 conserve, country, liberate, suffer

3.30 false

3.31 true

3.32 true

3.33 true

3.34 testimonials

3.35 glittering generalities

3.36 name calling

3.37 plain folks

3.38 bandwagon

SECTION ONE

1.1	c
1.2	a
1.3	e
1.4	f
1.5	b
1.6	d
1.7	31
1.8	free enterprise
1.9	railroads, mines
1.10	capitalism
1.11	Karl Marx
1.12	28
1.13	Adam Smith
1.14	T
1.15	c
1.16	•communism
	•mixed economy
	•capitalistic
1.17	c
1.18	a
1.19	e
1.20	f
1.21	d
1.22	b
1.23	employed
1.24	drop
1.25	Law of Supply and Demand
1.26	profit
1.27	higher
1.28	consumer, consumer
1.29	monopoly
1.30	T
1.31	c
1.32	d
1.33	b

1.34	f
1.35	a
1.36	e
1.37	boon
1.38	resources
1.39	vulcanizing
1.40	wage-price spiral
1.41	rise
1.42	T
1.43	T
1.44	F
1.45	T

1.46 •A labor force is all the people in your nation who are working or are seeking work.

•Descendants of the expelled Russian Mennonite farmers have continued to grow enormous crops of red wheat in the United States.

•It wouldn't make much sense to force an unskilled laborer to work in a surgical position.

1.47 •Your company's capital includes your rival company's water tower.

1.48 An economic condition in which the money supply is increasing faster than the supply of goods and services.

SECTION TWO

2.1	b		2.36	T
2.2	d		2.37	c,e
2.3	a		2.38	b
2.4	e		2.39	d
2.5	c		2.40	c
2.6	coupons		2.41	f
2.7	imports		2.42	a
2.8	competition		2.43	e
2.9	capital goods		2.44	h
2.10	prosperity		2.45	j
2.11	F		2.46	g
2.12	T		2.47	i
2.13	F		2.48	39.8
2.14	T		2.49	World, Africa
2.15	T		2.50	payment
2.16	a		2.51	Bartholomeu Diaz
2.17	b		2.52	Ferdinand Magellan
2.18	a		2.53	Christopher Columbus
2.19	e		2.54	gold
2.20	c		2.55	Adam Smith
2.21	d		2.56	•Trade was difficult.

2.22   i

2.23   f

2.24   j

2.25   k

2.26   g

2.27   h

2.28   trading centers

2.29   estates

2.30   Wilkinson

2.31   1936

2.32   CIO, AFL

2.33   F

2.34   F

2.35   F

2.56   •Trade was difficult.
•There was political division in the continent.
•Europe was a mass of small duchies and provinces.

2.57   b

2.58   c

2.59   T

2.60   T

SECTION THREE

3.1	c
3.2	b
3.3	d
3.4	i
3.5	a
3.6	e
3.7	h
3.8	j
3.9	f
3.10	g
3.11	yen
3.12	gold
3.13	dollar
3.14	buying power
3.15	F
3.16	T
3.17	F
3.18	c
3.19	e
3.20	b
3.21	a
3.22	d
3.23	value
3.24	1791
3.25	circulation
3.26	1800s
3.27	T
3.28	T
3.29	T
3.30	F
3.31	T
3.32	c

SECTION ONE

1.1 This concerns the day to day activities and decisions of the firm.

1.2 rob, Leviticus

1.3 entrepreneurship, operational management

1.4 profit, loss

1.5 respect

1.6 go-between or broker

1.7 communicate

1.8 fairness

1.9 masters, Master, fear

1.10 T

1.11 It is making decisions that affect the future of a business.

1.12 •top management
•board of directors

1.13 d

1.14 c

1.15 b

1.16 a

1.17 The business actually added less to the box - and kept the price the same. To make the bar thicker, they changed the instructions on the box to suggest that you use an 8-inch by 8-inch baking pan instead of their old directions which instructed you to use a 9-inch by 9-inch pan.

1.18 By hanging on to a car for ten years instead of making a new purchase with a trade-in every three years or so, a car owner can save $400,000 to $450,000 over a period of 40 years, even considering the higher costs for the repair of an older car.

1.19 return policy, warranty

1.20 a

1.21 c

1.22 b

1.23 beware

1.24 rebate

1.25 inventory

1.26 T

1.27 sheets and bedding

1.28 Internet

1.29 T

1.30 •If the car dealer will not or cannot show you the repair orders or identity of former owner, you should not buy the car.
•Have a mechanic friend look for hidden damage repairs on "new" (and used) cars.

1.31 At the local level, businesses must meet building standards, fire codes, and zoning laws. At the state level, many businesses are subject to extensive regulations such as licensing.

1.32 a

1.33 c

1.34 b

1.35 d

1.36 The Federal Communications Commission regulates radio and television to the extent of licensing stations and policing programming. The National Labor Relations Board regulates and oversees hiring practices. The Federal Aviation Administration regulates the airlines. The Federal Trade Commission regulates all credit transactions. The Securities and Exchange Commission regulates the stock market. The Federal Reserve Board regulates the banks. The Food and Drug Administration assesses all foods and drugs consumed. The Interstate Commerce Commission polices monopolistic practices.

1.37 safety, danger

1.38 electric companies

1.39 radio and television to the extent of licensing stations and policing programming.

1.40 money supply is increasing faster than the supply of goods and services.

1.41 wage-price spiral

1.42 debtors

1.43 F

1.44 T

SECTION TWO

2.1   c

2.2   a

2.3   b

2.4   e

2.5   d

2.6   f

2.7   h

2.8   g

2.9   i

2.10   Board of Governors

2.11   (any two of these): The Fed issues the nation's coin and paper currency. The U.S. Treasury, through its Bureau of the Mint and Bureau of Engraving and Printing, produces the nation's dollar and coin supply. The Fed Banks distribute the cash to financial institutions. As the currency works its way back to the Fed Banks, it is checked for wear and tear, and scrutinized for counterfeits. If the money is still in pretty good condition, it is goes back into circulation as banks and other institutions order new currency. Worn-out bills (bills usually have a life of 18 months) are destroyed.

2.12   credit, reserve

2.13   independent

2.14   T

2.15   F

2.16   F

2.17   T

2.18   harder to make loans.

2.19   securities

2.20   The Federal Reserve also rules on applications from banks who want to merge.

2.21   12

2.22   •open-market operations (purchase or sale of government securities)
      •change the discount rate
      •change reserve requirements

2.23   b

2.24   d

2.25   a

2.26   c

2.27   e

2.28   monopoly, control

2.29   mergers, production

2.30   board of directors

2.31   raise prices

2.32   1. Higher prices
      2. Lower quality
      3. Limitation or elimination on certain goods
      4. Poor service and attitude
      5. No rival competition or alternative markets.

2.33   incentive

2.34   F

2.35   F

2.36   T

2.37   T

SECTION THREE

3.1	proponents
3.2	IOU's
3.3	1978
3.4	purchasing, technological advances
3.5	e
3.6	b
3.7	a
3.8	c
3.9	d
3.10	f
3.11	4
3.12	F
3.13	F
3.14	T
3.15	T
3.16	F
3.17	T
3.18	e
3.19	f
3.20	d
3.21	c
3.22	b
3.23	a
3.24	bankruptcy court
3.25	reorganization
3.26	13
3.27	Matthew
3.28	infidel
3.29	T
3.30	T
3.31	F
3.32	T
3.33	T
3.34	F

SECTION ONE

1.1   1700s

1.2   Industrial Revolution

1.3   share

1.4   cash

1.5   not good enough

1.6   e

1.7   d

1.8   a

1.9   b

1.10   c

1.11   T

1.12   T

1.13   T

1.14   F

1.15   •In the early days of our nation, the colonial government was looking for a way to finance its wartime operations, so it sold bonds.
       •Traders would meet on what was once a farmer's market area known as Wall Street in New York.
       •In addition to bonds, the banks sold little parts of their banks to whomever had the money and the desire to own a share in the business.

1.16   services

1.17   purchasing

1.18   b

1.19   a

1.20   c

1.21   c

1.22   e

1.23   d

1.24   b

1.25   a

1.26   F

1.27   T

1.28   F

1.29   T

1.30   The first stock exchange was the New York Stock Exchange®

1.31   transaction

1.32   reports, house

1.33   commission

1.34   discount

1.35   c

1.36   b

1.37   a

1.38   T

1.39   T

1.40   F

1.41   floor of the New York Stock Exchange®

SECTION TWO

2.1   mutual funds

2.2   open mutual fund

2.3   service, competition

2.4   partnership, grow

2.5   gambling

2.6   d

2.7   c

2.8   b

2.9   a

2.10   T

2.11   T

2.12   T

2.13   F

2.14   profit

2.15
- When you buy the stock, you will be referred to as a shareholder or stockholder.
- If you don't see any profit from the company recently, that's a sign it may not be a good business for investment.
- One of the first rules that almost any investor will tell you is: Don't invest any money that you cannot afford to lose!

2.16   1929

2.17   1987

2.18   1932, 89

2.19   correction

2.20   c

2.21   a

2.22   b

2.23   T

2.24   F

2.25   T

2.26   point

2.27   1987

SECTION THREE

3.1	3
3.2	issue
3.3	AT&T®, Boeing®
3.4	dividend
3.5	letters
3.6	common, common, common
3.7	Blue chip stocks
3.8	b
3.9	a
3.10	d
3.11	c
3.12	T
3.13	T
3.14	F
3.15	T
3.16	T
3.17	tickers
3.18	hundreds, one hundred
3.19	volatility
3.20	day
3.21	profit
3.22	earnings, year
3.23	d
3.24	c
3.25	b
3.26	a
3.27	T
3.28	F
3.29	T
3.30	high, low and close

SECTION ONE

1.1	e	1.40	free period
1.2	a	1.41	due, give
1.3	c	1.42	prompt
1.4	d	1.43	b
1.5	b	1.44	b, c, d
1.6	Gross income	1.45	b, c
1.7	tithe	1.46	b
1.8	first fruits	1.47	e
1.9	Proverbs	1.48	T
1.10	Gross income	1.49	T
1.11	dwelling, reserves	1.50	T
1.12	more	1.51	c
1.13	expenses, income	1.52	d
1.14	paying yourself	1.53	e
1.15	month	1.54	f
1.16	account numbers	1.55	a
1.17	late fees	1.56	b
1.18	six	1.57	h
1.19	c	1.58	i
1.20	T	1.59	g
1.21	T	1.60	Proverbs 12:11
1.22	F	1.61	honorable, honorable
1.23	F	1.62	bank balance
1.24	T	1.63	a, b, d, f
1.25	e	1.64	c
1.26	c	1.65	F
1.27	d	1.66	F
1.28	a	1.67	b
1.29	b	1.68	d
1.30	increase	1.69	e
1.31	middle man	1.70	c
1.32	wisdom, not	1.71	a
1.33	warehouse club	1.72	down payment
1.34	e	1.73	power
1.35	T	1.74	standard
1.36	F	1.75	objective, subjective
1.37	T	1.76	T
1.38	credit limit	1.77	a, d
1.39	debt		

SECTION TWO

2.1	d		2.40	b
2.2	f		2.41	f
2.3	h		2.42	g
2.4	e		2.43	d
2.5	g		2.44	e
2.6	b		2.45	d
2.7	c		2.46	a
2.8	a		2.47	servicing fees
2.9	j		2.48	commercial real estate loan
2.10	k		2.49	Overextending
2.11	i		2.50	loan officer
2.12	c		2.51	unsecured
2.13	a, e		2.52	T
2.14	Proverbs 14:23		2.53	F
2.15	Federal Pell Grant		2.54	F
2.16	credit bureaus		2.55	b
2.17	unsubsidized		2.56	c
2.18	T		2.57	a
2.19	T		2.58	f
2.20	e		2.59	d
2.21	c		2.60	e
2.22	d		2.61	b
2.23	e		2.62	T
2.24	b		2.63	T
2.25	a		2.64	F
2.26	g		2.65	a, b, d, f
2.27	i		2.66	profit, service
2.28	f		2.67	payroll
2.29	h		2.68	paycheck
2.30	j		2.69	federal
2.31	installment payments		2.70	sponsors
2.32	earnings		2.71	members
2.33	pay tax		2.72	cooperative
2.34	withdrawal			
2.35	F			
2.36	F			
2.37	T			
2.38	c			
2.39	a			

SECTION THREE

3.1	ceilings	3.41	d
3.2	passbook	3.42	a
3.3	Bank Merger	3.43	b
3.4	Knights Templar	3.44	i
3.5	transfer	3.45	j
3.6	1600s	3.46	g
3.7	Personal Identification Number	3.47	h
3.8	T	3.48	f
3.9	F	3.49	c
3.10	d	3.50	1831
3.11	g	3.51	annual
3.12	e	3.52	buy a home
3.13	a	3.53	installment, home
3.14	b	3.54	serial
3.15	c	3.55	installment
3.16	f	3.56	59
3.17	F	3.57	d
3.18	F	3.58	e
3.19	T	3.59	a
3.20	d	3.60	b
3.21	c	3.61	f
3.22	d	3.62	g
3.23	f	3.63	c
3.24	a	3.64	fees
3.25	e	3.65	Travel/Money card
3.26	b	3.66	refund policy
3.27	$21.50, $20.00	3.67	1.5
3.28	transfer	3.68	Visa
3.29	foreign	3.69	cash
3.30	10	3.70	e
3.31	$200-$300	3.71	a, b, d
3.32	primary	3.72	T
3.33	T	3.73	F
3.34	T		
3.35	F		
3.36	T		
3.37	F		
3.38	T		
3.39	c		
3.40	e		

SECTION ONE

1.1	France	1.30	T
1.2	15, 11, 18	1.31	T
1.3	republic	1.32	F
1.4	stabilize, problems, markets, paperwork	1.33	Portugal
1.5	28, 34, 34	1.34	one-quarter
1.6	fluctuations	1.35	Frankfurt
1.7	Maine	1.36	Zurich
1.8	Greece	1.37	Victoria
1.9	2002	1.38	b
1.10	Netherlands	1.39	d
1.11	Greece	1.40	e
1.12	importing and exporting	1.41	c
1.13	Portugal	1.42	f
1.14	90%	1.43	a
1.15	f	1.44	g
1.16	d	1.45	a
1.17	c	1.46	e
1.18	e	1.47	c
1.19	b	1.48	d
1.20	a	1.49	T
1.21	d	1.50	F
1.22	c	1.51	T
1.23	b	1.52	T
1.24	a	1.53	T
1.25	F	1.54	F
1.26	T	1.55	T
1.27	T	1.56	F
1.28	F	1.57	F
1.29	F	1.58	T

SECTION TWO

2.1	Norway		2.38	g
2.2	subway		2.39	e
2.3	Fjords		2.40	d
2.4	Kyoto		2.41	h
2.5	70		2.42	i
2.6	Norway		2.43	a
2.7	sun		2.44	b
2.8	c		2.45	f
2.9	g		2.46	c
2.10	j		2.47	c
2.11	f		2.48	f
2.12	a		2.49	i
2.13	b		2.50	h
2.14	e		2.51	e
2.15	d		2.52	a
2.16	m		2.53	b
2.17	l		2.54	d
2.18	k		2.55	j
2.19	i		2.56	g
2.20	h		2.57	F
2.21	F		2.58	F
2.22	T		2.59	T
2.23	F		2.60	F
2.24	you don't get off the train		2.61	T
2.25	8,214,426		2.62	T
2.26	Oregon, Salem		2.63	F

2.26 Oregon, Salem
Maine, Augusta
Michigan, Lansing
Louisiana, Baton Rouge
North Carolina, Raleigh
Montana, Helena

2.27 49,401
2.28 Protestants
2.29 Northeast
2.30 Atlantic
2.31 Richmond
2.32 Louisiana or Arkansas
2.33 New York
2.34 Jackson
2.35 Dover
2.36 Oklahoma
2.37 Eastern

2.64 The Hawaiian islands became a U.S. territory in 1922.

SECTION THREE

3.1   1994
3.2   privatizing
3.3   Pacific Ocean
3.4   Caribbean Sea
3.5   Mexico
3.6   tariffs
3.7   Belize
3.8   7
3.9   -84° *or* 84 degrees below zero
3.10   g
3.11   f
3.12   e
3.13   b
3.14   d
3.15   a
3.16   j
3.17   h
3.18   i
3.19   c
3.20   F
3.21   T
3.22   F
3.23   British Columbia
3.24   •Canada has 10 provinces and 3
        territories.
        •Abundant natural resources and a
        massive skilled labor force are two
        advantages that promise Canada better
        economic prospects ahead.
        •Tijuana is north of Mexico City.
        •Alberta shares a border with British
        Columbia.
        •The Yukon and the American state of
        Alaska share a border.
3.25   five
3.26   an Israeli
3.27   Haifa
3.28   Balfour
3.29   muezzin
3.30   1948
3.31   e
3.32   h
3.33   j
3.34   i
3.35   b
3.36   a

3.37   c
3.38   g
3.39   d
3.40   l
3.41   k
3.42   f
3.43   T
3.44   F
3.45   Pakistan
3.46   •Lebanon and Syria are neighboring
        countries.
        •Israel's Prime Minister Yitzak Rabin
        was assassinated in 1994 by another
        Israeli.
3.47   7
        5
        6
        4
        1
        2
        3
3.48   zayat
3.49   Burma, Canada, Tunisia
3.50   1300s
3.51   martyr
3.52   Acts chapter 11
3.53   e
3.54   c
3.55   a
3.56   b
3.57   d
3.58   c
3.59   d
3.60   b
3.61   a
3.62   F
3.63   T
3.64   Turkey
3.65   •When George Müller was a student at
        the University of Halle, he met a number
        of Christians who impressed him.
        •Evan Roberts was so overcome with
        audible prayer in his apartment that his
        landlady thought he had gone mad.
        •Ignatius' home city of Antioch is
        located in modern-day Turkey.

SELF TEST 1

1.01	a
1.02	f
1.03	e
1.04	d
1.05	b
1.06	c
1.07	T
1.08	T
1.09	F
1.010	T
1.011	tangible, intangible
1.012	Aristotle
1.013	Bureaucracy
1.014	they enforce rules that control conduct within a population
1.015	oversee business
1.016	pluralism
1.017	polity
1.018	morality
1.019	jurisdiction
1.020	racial, ethnic, business
1.021	allowing private business and free speech.
1.022	dictator
1.023	(either): Idi Amin of Uganda, Saddam Hussein
1.024	bureaucracy
1.025	Habeas Corpus
1.026	control all branches of government.
1.027	king
1.028	foreign exchange

SELF TEST 2

2.01	PRI, 70
2.02	president
2.03	the Senate, House of Representatives
2.04	Constitution
2.05	veto
2.06	"House of Commons," "House of Lords"
2.07	Prime Minister
2.08	Parliament
2.09	five
2.010	Edward II, Richard II
2.011	six
2.012	T
2.013	F
2.014	F
2.015	Romans chapter 13
2.016	they are both appointed for life.

SELF TEST 3

3.01	Khmer Rouge
3.02	(answers may vary)
3.03	the Communist party
3.04-3.08	(any five of the following):France, Japan, Belgium, Italy, Denmark, Sri Lanka
3.09	liberal
3.010	The Tenure of Kings and Magistrates
3.011	salvation
3.012	*Summa Theologica*
3.013	culture
3.014	T
3.015	T
3.016	1 Timothy 2:1-4
3.017	atrocity
3.018	• he taught that people should find their "function." • Alexander the Great was a pupil of his.
3.019	Engels once personally tutored Karl Marx.
3.020	*Summa Doxologica*

SELF TEST 1

1.01	f
1.02	a
1.03	c
1.04	e
1.05	d
1.06	b
1.07	F
1.08	T
1.09	F
1.010	T
1.011	T
1.012	criminal
1.013	correcting a wrong that was done.
1.014	endowed, unalienable
1.015	"domestic tranquility"
1.016	Bill of Rights
1.017	10
1.018	state government
1.019	president, vice president
1.020	assemble
1.021	redress
1.022	not allowing excessive bail or punishment
1.023	(any 2 of the 3): rights, immunities, freedoms
1.024	fourth
1.025	sixth
1.026	listed, right
1.027	making laws and enforcing them
1.028	Constitution
1.029	treaties
1.030	Congress may not prevent a religion from free exercise
1.031	1962
1.032	It gives a general outline of information in electing the president of the United States.
1.033	Congress has the right to limit the free practice of religion.
1.034	the right to keep and bear arms.

SELF TEST 2

2.01	interpret	2.023	• National Security Council
2.02	executive, legislative, judicial		• Office of Policy Development
2.03	diplomatic relations	2.024	d
2.04	2	2.025	f
2.05	nullify	2.026	a
2.06	Constitution	2.027	e
2.07	divided government	2.028	b
2.08	president pro tempore	2.029	c
2.09	Article I	2.030	• The Claims Court is a part of the judiciary system.
2.010	most recent U.S. Census		• Nine justices serve in the Supreme Court.
2.011	T		• There are 12 courts of appeal in the judiciary system.
2.012	F		• Federal judges on the Supreme Court serve for life.
2.013	F		
2.014	T		
2.015	F		
2.016	F		
2.017	T	2.031	e
2.018	T	2.032	f
2.019	T	2.033	d
2.020	T	2.034	a
2.021	T	2.035	b
2.022	The executive branch is one of the three branches of the U.S. government; this branch mainly interprets the federal laws and upholds or negates them.	2.036	c

SELF TEST 3

3.01	concurrence	3.014	If a bill is approved by the committee and has survived a Senate vote, the bill will go to the House of Representatives.
3.02	versions		
3.03	Hearings		
3.04	draft		
3.05	introduce	3.015	H.R. signifies a House bill and S. a Senate Bill
3.06	changes, amendments		
3.07	voted it down	3.016	Ordering a bill reported: A subcommittee reads its recommendation to both houses of Congress.
3.08	the subcommittee lets it sit and does nothing.		
3.09	House		
3.010	10	3.017	(ALL the boxes are NOT TRUE)
3.011	F	3.018	a
3.012	T	3.019	d
3.013	T	3.020	b
		3.021	c

SELF TEST 1

1.01	e	1.027	c
1.02	f	1.028	a
1.03	d	1.029	b
1.04	a	1.030	d
1.05	b	1.031	e
1.06	c	1.032	T
1.07	Democratic	1.033	F
1.08	central	1.034	T
1.09	Breckinridge, Douglas	1.035	T
1.010	Grover Cleveland, Woodrow Wilson	1.036	T

1.011   (any 5): Progressive Party, Bull
Moose Party, Dixiecrats Party,
American Independent Party,
Liberal Republicans Party, Gold
Democrats Party, Greenback Party,
Socialist Party, Social Workers Party,
Prohibition Party, American
Communist Party, New Party,
Natural Law Party, United We
Stand Party, Reform Party,
Libertarian Party, The Green Party,
The US Taxpayers Party,
Communist Party U.S.A.

1.037	T
1.038	T
1.039	T
1.040	F
1.041	F
1.042	F
1.043	the powers the constitution delegated to it

1.044   •The Republican Party began as a
series of anti-slavery political
meetings held in the midwest in
1854.
•During the election of 1824,
Andrew Jackson won the most
electoral votes, but not the majority
needed to be elected president.
•The Anti-Federalist would limit
the federal government strictly to
the powers the constitution
delegated to it.
•Third parties play a highly
important role in the strengthening
the two major parties

1.012	incumbent
1.013	has only one goal
1.014	American Communist Party
1.015	specific group of people
1.016	b
1.017	a
1.018	d
1.019	c
1.020	loose construction
1.021	federal government
1.022	strict construction
1.023	Democratic, Republican
1.024	1848

1.045   •The Democrats blamed the
Republicans for the Stock Market
crash of 1929.
•The Democrats won the presidency
in the 90s but lost control of the
Congress.
•The "Era of Good feelings" was a
period from 1816-1824 where there
was only one political party: the
Democrat-Republicans.

1.025   (any): Jackson, Van Buren, Polk,
Pierce, Buchanan, Cleveland,
Wilson, Tyler, Roosevelt, Truman,
Kennedy, Johnson, Carter, Clinton

1.026   (any): Lincoln, Grant, Hayes,
Harrison, Mckinley, Ford, Johnson,
Garfield, Hoover, Arthur, Roosevelt,
Taft, Harding, Coolidge,
Eisenhower, Nixon, Reagan, Bush

1.046	all of the above
1.047	d

1.048	a		1.052	f
1.049	b		1.053	c
1.050	h		1.054	e
1.051	g			

SELF TEST 2

2.01	T		2.014	b
2.02	T		2.015	a
2.03	F		2.016	d
2.04	T		2.017	c
2.05	Democratic		2.018	
2.06	captain, committeeman			
2.07	(private) donations			
2.08	Declaration, payment, petition			
2.09	controversial			
2.010	*The Republican*			
2.011	conducting a census			
2.012	George Bush			
2.013	national committee			

2.018
- The federal power of the country is known as the central government.
- Ronald Reagan was praised for making the economy strong during the 80s.
- Phil Gramm spent over 9 million dollars in his presidential bid in 1996.

SELF TEST 3

3.01	orally		3.025	it was invented in 1898
3.02	single		3.026	e
3.03	column		3.027	b
3.04	block		3.028	c
3.05	conduct		3.029	d
3.06	400		3.030	a
3.07	county supervisors, district election board		3.031	
3.08	business			
3.09	mail			
3.010	notary public, clerk			
3.011	secret ballot			
3.012	split ticket			
3.013	candidate			
3.014	short		3.032	recount
3.015	four		3.033	
3.016	unopposed			
3.017	long ballot			
3.018	T			
3.019	T			
3.020	T			
3.021	F			
3.022	F			
3.023	T			
3.024	T			

3.031
- A school is an acceptable building used for a polling place.
- A fire station is an acceptable building used for a polling place.
- A church is an acceptable building used for a polling place.
- A library is an acceptable building used for a polling place.

3.033
- You must be 18 years of age.
- You must vote in your designated precinct.
- There will be a ballot box to receive your voting ballot, if a ballot is used.
- Your name and address will be verified at a registration table.

SELF TEST 1

1.01	Proverbs 29:18	1.025	b
1.02	[the] Concilum Plebus	1.026	e
		1.027	d
1.03	production, sustenance	1.028	a
		1.029	c
1.04	Athens	1.030	Etrusians, Flavians
1.05	oligarchy	1.031	A dominating nation with
1.06	750 B.C.		extensive territories and a
1.07	vision		powerful ruler such as Rome's is
1.08	27		known as an empire.
1.09	450 B.C.	1.032	c
1.010	true	1.033	e
1.011	true	1.034	b
1.012	true	1.035	f
1.013	false	1.036	a
1.014	false	1.037	d
1.015	false		

1.016 true

1.017 c

1.018 f

1.019 e

1.020 a

1.021 d

1.022 b

1.023
- Safety is a priority.
- Leadership is needed
- Production and sustenance should be provided daily.
- The government should have a goal.
- Law and order should be maintained.

1.024 Sparta's main strength was in its navy.

1.038
- In Rome, only men with money and property could vote.
- In Greece all free men were allowed to vote.
- In the Roman Senate, the most powerful part of the government, all senators were patricians.

1.039 b

1.040 e

1.041 d

1.042 a

1.043 c

SELF TEST 2

2.01	true
2.02	false
2.03	true
2.04	false
2.05	true
2.06	true
2.07	false
2.08	b
2.09	e
2.010	d
2.011	a
2.012	c

2.013 Feudalism is a system of cooperation among peoples which was basically an exchange of gold for protection.

2.014 King John of England was a vassal himself who refused some of the rulings of Ferdinand and war broke out between the factions.

2.015	b
2.016	d
2.017	subinfeudation
2.018	Judges
2.019	my son
2.020	Midianites
2.021	Exodus
2.022	death

2.023 John Jay
Alexander Hamilton
James Madison

2.024 opportunity for education,
equality before the law,
the citizens freedom,
voting rights

2.025	h
2.026	g
2.027	f
2.028	a
2.029	c
2.030	d
2.031	e
2.032	b

2.033 The system of cooperation known as feudalism ended around the 15 century.

2.034 We still carry the idea of one presiding authority, a judge, and peers who will help in the decision making process. A Vassal would answer a summons.

SELF TEST 3

3.01   true

3.02   false

3.03   true

3.04   true

3.05   true

3.06   true

3.07   c

3.08   d

3.09   e

3.010   a

3.011   b

3.012   Might makes right or Ruling by
         Strength

3.013   World War II

3.014   rods

3.015   freedom of worship,
         cultural pursuits

3.016   "final solution"

3.017   chancellor

3.018   Fascists usually gain power after
         a country's economic collapse.

3.019   •The Axis powers were made up
          of a coalition of countries that
          opposed the Allied powers in
          World War II.

         •Hitler's Nazi Party carried many
          traits of the fascist beliefs.

3.020   c

3.021   Massive fascist propaganda
         campaigns sweep the country in
         order to promote freedom of
         religion.

SELF TEST 1

1.01	d	1.034	false	
1.02	c	1.035	true	
1.03	b	1.036	false	
1.04	e	1.037	true	
1.05	a	1.038	false	
1.06	l	1.039	true	

1.07   i

1.08   f

1.09   g

1.010   j

1.011   h

1.012   k

1.013   o

1.014   n

1.015   q

1.016   m

1.017   p

1.018   fathers, nation

1.019   parochial schools

1.020   1500s

1.021   neutrality

1.022   American Civil Liberties Union

1.023   15th

1.024   Romans 10:12

1.025   segregation

1.026   social rewards

1.027   freedom

1.028   love

1.029   false

1.030   true

1.031   true

1.032   true

1.033   true

1.040   •The government is forbidden to establish a religion
•The government is forbidden to interfere with or regulate religion.

1.041   Slavery was an established institution until the Twelfth Amendment was ratified on December 18, 1865.

1.042   e

1.043   b

1.044   b

1.045   c

1.046   It was a nonviolent demonstration in the form of civil rights rally held in Washington, D.C. on August 28, 1963 and where some 200,000 people (African American and White), who supported the cause of equal rights, peacefully illustrated their impatience with slow government action concerning civil rights. A key speaker for the rally was Dr. Martin Luther King.

1.047   We are to put away strife and pride and esteem others higher than ourselves.

SELF TEST 2

2.01	b
2.02	d
2.03	e
2.04	a
2.05	c
2.06	T
2.07	F
2.08	T
2.09	F
2.010	T
2.011	T
2.012	F
2.013	particular issue
2.014	facts

2.015	Gallup, Harris
2.016	one-man
2.017	know, opinion
2.018	advertisers
2.019	Newsweek
2.020	audio, visual
2.021	editors
2.022	"Meet the Press," "Face the Nation"
2.023	any six: newspapers, television, movies, magazines, radio, propaganda, family, church, friends, motion pictures
2.024	d

SELF TEST 3

3.01	c
3.02	a
3.03	d
3.04	e
3.05	b
3.06	g
3.07	i
3.08	h
3.09	f
3.010	k
3.011	l
3.012	m
3.013	n
3.014	j
3.015	Treasury
3.016	conserve, liberate

3.017	"Boy's State," "Boy's Nation," "Girl's State"
3.018	Judas
3.019	"Lincoln Day Dinner," "Jackson Day Dinner"
3.020	plain folks
3.021	5:9
3.022	T
3.023	T
3.024	F
3.025	F
3.026	F
3.027	a
3.028	b
3.029	e

SELF TEST 1

1.01	d		1.017	T
1.02	c		1.018	T
1.03	a		1.019	T
1.04	e		1.020	F
1.05	b		1.021	T
1.06	wheat		1.022	F
1.07	higher		1.023	F
1.08	boon		1.024	F
1.09	resources		1.025	T
1.010	money		1.026	T
1.011	wage-price spiral		1.027	T
1.012	rise		1.028	b, c, d
1.013	vulcanizing		1.029	a, c, e
1.014	railroads, mines		1.030	d
1.015	T		1.031	e
1.016	F		1.032	a, b, d

SELF TEST 2

2.01	b		2.023	gold
2.02	d		2.024	Adam Smith
2.03	a		2.025	raw materials
2.04	c		2.026	sales tactic
2.05	f		2.027	prosperity
2.06	h		2.028	T
2.07	i		2.029	F
2.08	e		2.030	T
2.09	g		2.031	T
2.010	j		2.032	T
2.011	k		2.033	T
2.012	l		2.034	T
2.013	o		2.035	T
2.014	q		2.036	F
2.015	p		2.037	T
2.016	m		2.038	T
2.017	n		2.039	a, b, c, d, e, f
2.018	work		2.040	b, c, e
2.019	Wilkinson		2.041	b
2.020	CIO, AFL		2.042	a
2.021	World, Africa		2.043	c
2.022	medium of exchange		2.044	c, e

SELF TEST 3

3.01	b
3.02	a
3.03	d
3.04	e
3.05	c
3.06	g
3.07	j
3.08	h
3.09	f
3.010	i
3.011	m
3.012	l
3.013	o
3.014	k
3.015	n
3.016	yen
3.017	Greenbacks
3.018	1800s
3.019	postal currency
3.020	gold
3.021	1791
3.022	monetary policy
3.023	T
3.024	F
3.025	F
3.026	T
3.027	F
3.028	F
3.029	T
3.030	a, f

SELF TEST 1

1.01	e
1.02	d
1.03	j
1.04	a
1.05	c
1.06	b
1.07	i
1.08	h
1.09	f
1.010	g
1.011	Acting ethically
1.012	By hanging on to a car for ten years instead of making a new purchase with a trade-in every three years or so, a car owner can save $400,000 to $450,000 over a period of 40 years, even considering the higher costs for the repair of an older car.
1.013	return policy, warranty
1.014	Internet
1.015	c
1.016	a
1.017	d
1.018	b
1.019	rebate
1.020	inventory
1.021	rob, Leviticus
1.022	entrepreneurship, operational management
1.023	go-between or broker
1.024	communicate
1.025	fairness
1.026	masters, Master, fear
1.027	inflation
1.028	safety, trust, danger
1.029	electric companies
1.030	stock market
1.031	F
1.032	T
1.033	F
1.034	T
1.035	T
1.036	T

1.037
- the business actually added less to the box and kept the price the same.

1.038
- If the car dealer will not or cannot show you the repair orders or identity of former owner, you should not buy the car.
- Have a mechanic friend look for hidden damage repairs on "new" (and used) cars.

1.039 the day-to-day operation of a business

1.040
- top management
- board of directors

1.041 At the local level, businesses must meet government-set billing rates.

1.042 wage price spiral

1.043 debtors

1.044
- The Federal Communications Commission regulates radio and television to the extent of licensing stations and policing programming.
- The Federal Aviation Administration regulates the airlines.
- The Securities and Exchange Commission regulates the stock market.
- The Interstate Commerce Commission polices monopolistic practices.
- The Food and Drug Administration assesses all foods and drugs consumed.

SELF TEST 2

2.01   d

2.02   c

2.03   a

2.04   b

2.05   stock market

2.06   electric companies

2.07   incentive

2.08   Clayton Antitrust Act

2.09   a

2.010   c

2.011   b

2.012   d

2.013   d

2.014   e

2.015   a

2.016   c

2.017   b

2.018   f

2.019   securities

2.020   Board of Governors

2.021   credit, reserve

2.022   independent

2.023   checking

2.024   c

2.025   e

2.026   d

2.027   b

2.028   a

2.029   raise prices

2.030   T

2.031   T

2.032   T

2.033   T

2.034   T

2.035   •Higher prices
•No rival competition or alternative markets
•Lower quality
•Limitation or elimination of certain goods
•Poor service and attitude

2.036   •Monopolies are judged by how strong the competition is between the companies.
•The Fed issues the nation's coin and paper currency.
•Trusts were unofficial mergers formed to control prices and production in the marketplace.

2.037   The Fed was started in 1933.

2.038   •One of the largest divestitures in American history occurred when the U.S. Government ruled that the AT&T® Corporation was a monopoly that must be divided so that the telephone market might be more competitive.
•The Federal Aviation Administration regulates the airlines.
•The Securities and Exchange Commission regulates the stock market.
•The Interstate Commerce Commission polices monopolistic practices.

2.039   •open-market operations (purchase or sale of government securities).
•change the discount rate.
•change reserve requirements.

SELF TEST 3

3.01	purchasing, technological advances	3.044	T
3.02	d	3.045	T
3.03	c	3.046	T
3.04	e	3.047	T
3.05	f	3.048	T
3.06	b	3.049	T
3.07	a	3.050	F
3.08	4	3.051	T
3.09	a	3.052	a
3.010	b	3.053	b
3.011	f	3.054	c
3.012	d	3.055	d
3.013	e	3.056	e

3.014   c

3.015   liquidation

3.016   bankruptcy court

3.017   Romans 13:8

3.018   Matthew

3.019   infidel

3.020   stock market

3.021   electric companies

3.022   incentive

3.023   Clayton Antitrust Act

3.024   a

3.025   d

3.026   b

3.027   c

3.028   e

3.029   d

3.030   c

3.031   a

3.032   b

3.033   f

3.034   Board of Governors

3.035   credit, reserve

3.036   independent

3.037   borrows from

3.038   d

3.039   c

3.040   b

3.041   e

3.042   a

3.043   raise prices

3.057
- After passage of the 1996 deregulation law, the Baby Bells started merging with each other, and two of them attempted to re-merge into AT&T®.
- A lone utility company, Detroit Edison and Consumers Power, faced new competition as deregulation gave people a choice between utility companies. The company tried to battle the act by asking for funds to cover "stranded costs" and lost income once the process was underway, but the deregulation went through.

3.058   Deregulated Investor Owned Utilities are known as IOU's.

3.059
- A Chapter 7 bankruptcy is known as a "straight liquidation."
- Financial responsibility in the home is found in the Bible passage of 1 Timothy 5:8.
- A Chapter 13 bankruptcy filing is called a reorganization.

3.060
- No rival competition or alternative markets
- Lower quality
- Limitation or elimination of certain goods
- Poor service and attitude
- Higher prices

SELF TEST 3 continued

3.061   •Monopolies are judged by how
        strong the competition is between
        the companies.
        •In 1911 the Standard Oil Company
        was divided into more than 30
        separate companies.
        •The Fed issues the nation's coin
        and paper currency.
        •Trusts are agreed-upon unofficial
        mergers formed to control prices
        and production in the
        marketplace.

3.062   The Fed was started in 1933.

3.063   •One of the largest divestitures in
        American history occurred when
        the U.S. Government ruled that
        the AT&T® Corporation was a
        monopoly that must be divided so
        that the telephone market might
        be more competitive.
        •Week by week the finances in this
        country can change, so the selling
        and buying of securities helps
        maintain equilibrium.

3.064   •open-market operations (purchase
        or sale of government securities)
        •change the discount rate
        •change reserve requirements

SELF TEST 1

1.01	floor
1.02	broker
1.03	Belgium
1.04	AMEX®
1.05	share
1.06	Industrial Revolution
1.07	share
1.08	cash
1.09	not good enough
1.010	prospectus
1.011	services or commission
1.012	purchasing
1.013	reports, house
1.014	employee
1.015	commission
1.016	b
1.017	a
1.018	c
1.019	a
1.020	b
1.021	e
1.022	d
1.023	c
1.024	a
1.025	b
1.026	d
1.027	e
1.028	c
1.029	F
1.030	T
1.031	T
1.032	T
1.033	transaction

1.034
- The New York Stock Exchange® is also known by its initials, NYSE®.
- England's first stock exchange originated in 1773.
- The New York Stock Exchange® began with a handful of men standing in front of a buttonwood tree near the Trinity Church in East Manhattan during the American Revolution.

1.035 A broker is the person who will do the actual purchasing of the stocks for you.

1.036
- When you purchase a share, you have purchased a little piece of the company.
- People will subscribe to publications such as Barron's® or The Wall Street Journal® to get information on investing more wisely.
- Mattel®, as well as thousands of other companies, offers the opportunity to buy a part of their company by selling shares.
- A prospectus is a plan of a new business or financial endeavor, including how much capital is needed in order to be a shareholder, and the profits that an investor may realize.

SELF TEST 2

2.01   profit

2.02   climb

2.03   product

2.04   competition

2.05   stockholder

2.06   skeptical

2.07   gambling

2.08   lose

2.09   1929

2.010   1932, 89

2.011   Crash

2.012   c

2.013   b

2.014   d

2.015   a

2.016   f

2.017   g

2.018   e

2.019   T

2.020   T

2.021   T

2.022   F

2.023   T

2.024   mutual funds

2.025
- Buying stock should be equated with buying into a partnership of a business - after all, your money is going into a corporation that will try to use it to grow.
- If the company has been making a good profit against competition, you may continue to see that profit grow, and that is a good sign for investing.

2.026   point

2.027   Investors' fears become so powerful that increased movement on the stock exchange occurs, causing a financial panic.

SELF TEST 3

3.01   high, low and close

3.02   hundreds

3.03   one hundred

3.04   volatility

3.05   day

3.06   z

3.07   margin, risk

3.08   earnings, year

3.09   AT&T®, Boeing®

3.010   dividend

3.011   common, common, common

3.012   Blue chip stocks

3.013   k

3.014   c

3.015   e

3.016   m

3.017   h

3.018   a

3.019   n

3.020   d

3.021   o

3.022   p

3.023   g

3.024   f

3.025   b

3.026   i

3.027   j

3.028   l

3.029   q

3.030   T

3.031   F

3.032   T

3.033   T

3.034   F

3.035   T

3.036   tickers

3.037
- The S&P® list contains the 500 largest publicly held companies.
- Your portfolio is all of the various stocks or bonds that you, as an investor, hold.
- Standard & Poor's® 500 is a type of stock index favored by professionals because it includes a far wider range of public companies than the Dow Jones℠ industrial average does.
- A preferred stock is a financial return that has a set limit.

SELF TEST 1

1.01	b		1.036	T
1.02	e		1.037	T
1.03	a		1.038	T
1.04	d		1.039	F
1.05	c		1.040	T
1.06	h		1.041	T
1.07	i		1.042	T
1.08	j		1.043	T
1.09	f		1.044	b
1.010	g		1.045	b
1.011	n		1.046	a, d
1.012	m			
1.013	p			
1.014	l			
1.015	o			
1.016	k			
1.017	Proverbs 3:9-10			
1.018	impulse buying			
1.019	increase, savings			
1.020	late fees			
1.021	warehouse club			
1.022	honorable, honorable			
1.023	bank balance			
1.024	gross income			
1.025	more			
1.026	expenses, income			
1.027	paying yourself			
1.028	account numbers			
1.029	total			
1.030	middle man			
1.031	power			
1.032	standard			
1.033	objective, subjective			
1.034	b			
1.035	a, b, d, e, g			

SELF TEST 2

2.01	c		2.036	b, c, d
2.02	a		2.037	a, b, d, f
2.03	b		2.038	b, c
2.04	d		2.039	d
2.05	f		2.040	a
2.06	g		2.041	b
2.07	e			
2.08	i			
2.09	h			
2.010	defer			
2.011	deferment			
2.012	credit bureaus			
2.013	education			
2.014	credit limit			
2.015	due, give			
2.016	plan			
2.017	profit, service			
2.018	federal			
2.019	sponsors			
2.020	cooperative			
2.021	commercial real estate loan			
2.022	loan officer			
2.023	unsecured			
2.024	T			
2.025	T			
2.026	F			
2.027	T			
2.028	T			
2.029	T			
2.030	T			
2.031	T			
2.032	T			
2.033	T			
2.034	F			
2.035	c			

SELF TEST 3

3.01	ceilings
3.02	Bank Merger
3.03	1600s
3.04	Personal Identification Number
3.05	$21.50, $20.00
3.06	foreign
3.07	$200-$300
3.08	primary
3.09	1831
3.010	annual
3.011	installment, home
3.012	59
3.013	refund policy
3.014	1.5
3.015	Visa
3.016	cash
3.017	T
3.018	F
3.019	F
3.020	T
3.021	F
3.022	T
3.023	T
3.024	F
3.025	a
3.026	b
3.027	d
3.028	c
3.029	f
3.030	e
3.031	h
3.032	g

SELF TEST 1

1.01	France		1.035	i
1.02	London		1.036	h
1.03	stabilize, problems, markets,		1.037	d
	paperwork		1.038	j
1.04	Euroland		1.039	c
1.05	fluctuations		1.040	g
1.06	water		1.041	F
1.07	London		1.042	T
1.08	Netherlands		1.043	T
1.09	Greece		1.044	F
1.010	Netherlands		1.045	F
1.011	importing, exporting		1.046	F
1.012	Portugal		1.047	T
1.013	one-quarter		1.048	F
1.014	Frauminster, Zurich		1.049	T
1.015	Frankfurt		1.050	F
1.016	Victoria		1.051	F
1.017	18			
1.018	d			
1.019	g			
1.020	h			
1.021	l			
1.022	e			
1.023	b			
1.024	f			
1.025	k			
1.026	j			
1.027	m			
1.028	a			
1.029	c			
1.030	i			
1.031	a			
1.032	e			
1.033	b			
1.034	f			

SELF TEST 2

2.01	8,214,426		2.043	i
2.02	49,401		2.044	a
2.03	Protestants		2.045	f
2.04	Northeast		2.046	d
2.05	Jackson		2.047	h
2.06	three		2.048	T
2.07	Dover		2.049	T
2.08	Oklahoma		2.050	F
2.09	Eastern		2.051	F
2.010	Norway		2.052	T
2.011	Montana		2.053	F
2.012	fjords		2.054	T
2.013	Kyoto		2.055	F
2.014	70		2.056	F
2.015	sun		2.057	T
2.016	j		2.058	F
2.017	e		2.059	a
2.018	d		2.060	Oregon, Salem
2.019	a			Maine, Augusta
2.020	h			Michigan, Lansing
2.021	l			Louisiana, Baton Rouge
2.022	g			North Carolina, Raleigh
2.023	c			Montana, Helena
2.024	b		2.061	Columbus
2.025	m			Annapolis
2.026	i			Wisconsin
2.027	k			Washington
2.028	f		2.062	d
2.029	j		2.063	c
2.030	g			
2.031	i			
2.032	h			
2.033	f			
2.034	e			
2.035	b			
2.036	a			
2.037	d			
2.038	c			
2.039	i			
2.040	f			
2.041	c			
2.042	g			

SELF TEST 3

3.01	1994	3.048	d
3.02	privatizing	3.049	b
3.03	Pacific Ocean	3.050	c
3.04	Caribbean Sea	3.051	a
3.05	Gulf of Mexico	3.052	F
3.06	tariffs	3.053	T
3.07	Belize	3.054	F
3.08	7%	3.055	T
3.09	-84° *or* 84 degrees below zero	3.056	F
3.010	seven	3.057	F
3.011	an Israeli	3.058	T
3.012	Haifa	3.059	British Columbia
3.013	Balfour	3.060	•Canada has 10 provinces and 2 territories.
3.014	muezzin		•Abundant natural resources and a massive skilled labor force are two advantages that promise Canada better economic prospects ahead.
3.015	1948		
3.016	zayat		
3.017	Africa, Asia		
3.018	1300s		•Tijuana is north of Mexico City.
3.019	martyr		•Alberta shares a border with British Columbia.
3.020	Acts chapter 11		
3.021	g		•The Yukon and the American state of Alaska share a border.
3.022	h		
3.023	b	3.061	Pakistan
3.024	j	3.062	•Lebanon and Syria are neighboring countries.
3.025	e		
3.026	c		•Canaan was the name given to the region of Israel during Old Testament times.
3.027	a		
3.028	f		
3.029	i	3.063	Turkey
3.030	d	3.064	•When George Müller was a student at the University of Halle, he met a number of Christians who impressed him.
3.031	i		
3.032	g		
3.033	b		
3.034	e		•Evan Roberts was so overcome with audible prayer in his apartment that his landlady thought he had gone mad.
3.035	k		
3.036	c		
3.037	h		
3.038	l		•Ignatius' home city of Antioch is located in modern-day Turkey.
3.039	j		
3.040	a		
3.041	f	3.065	2
3.042	d		1
3.043	d		5
3.044	e		3
3.045	c		7
3.046	a		4
3.047	b		6

1. T
2. F
3. T
4. F
5. T
6. T
7. T
8. F
9. PRI, 70
10. tangible, intangible
11. dictator
12. Constitution
13. Communist
14. function
15. *The Tenure of Kings and Magistrates*
16. culture
17. Aristotle
18. morality
19. Senate, House of Representatives
20. they enforce rules that control conduct within a population
21. atrocity
22. f
23. e
24. d
25. a
26. b
27. c
28. pluralism
29. (any four of the following): France, Belgium, Italy, Sri Lanka, Japan, Denmark
30. *Das Kapital, The Communist Manifesto*

1. T
2. T
3. F
4. T
5. F
6. F
7. F
8. T
9. T
10. T
11. T
12. versions
13. debating
14. the subcommittee lets it set and does nothing
15. 13
16. Executive, Legislative, Judicial
17. 2
18. Constitution
19. president pro tempore
20. census
21. criminal
22. endowed, unalienable
23. prayer
24. president
25. not allowing excessive bail or punishment
26. Fourth
27. listed, right
28. public safety
29. Constitution or acts of Congress
30. a
31. b
32. d
33. c
34. Ordering a bill reported: A subcommittee reads its recommendation to both houses of Congress
35. The executive branch is one of the three branches of the U.S. government; this branch mainly interprets the federal laws and upholds or negates them.
36.
   - The claims court is a part of the judiciary system.
   - Nine justices serve in the Supreme Court.
   - There are 12 courts of appeal in the judiciary system.
   - Federal judges on the Supreme Court serve for life.
37. b
38. c
39. a
40. Congress may not create a religion.
41. Congress has the right to limit the free practice of religion.

1. partisan politics
2. loose construction
3. (any 6) Lincoln, Andrew Johnson, Grant, Hayes, Garfield, Arthur, Harrison, McKinley, Theodore Roosevelt, Taft, Harding, Coolidge, Hoover, Eisenhower, Nixon, Ford, Reagan, Bush
4. Jimmy Carter
5. Australian
6. central
7. Grover Cleveland, Woodrow Wilson
8. incumbent
9. specific groups of people
10. federal government
11. captain, committeeman
12. national
13. orally
14. column
15. county supervisors, district election board
16. mail
17. secret ballot
18. short
19. long ballot
20. T
21. T
22. F
23. T
24. F
25. T
26. F
27. F
28. T
29. T
30. T
31. registering to vote with the party you wish to join
32. every four years

33.
    - if most members in the Congress from his states are Republican
    - if his state has a Republican governor
    - his state cast electoral votes in the last election for the Republican candidate
34. e
35. f
36. a
37. c
38. b
39. g
40. d
41. h
42. i
43. would limit the federal government strictly to the powers the constitution delegated to it
44. calling for a recount
45. e
46. a
47. b
48. c
49. f
50. d
51. The federal power of the country is known as the central government
52.
    - To vote a split ticket requires knowledge of the qualifications of every candidate.
    - In order to vote, you must be 18 years of age and must vote in your designated precinct.
    - One way to cut down on the number of elections would be to lengthen the term of office for elected officials.
    - Your name and address will be verified at the registration table.
    - The president and vice president are elected once every four years

1. true
2. true
3. false
4. false
5. false
6. true
7. false
8. true
9. true
10. Proverbs 29:18
11. Production and sustenance
12. oligarchy
13. 27
14. Diotrepehes
15. 12
16. my son
17. Exodus
18. two-year
19. Might makes right or Rule by Strength
20. rods, axes
21. "final solution"
22. tyrants
23. c
24. b
25. d
26. a
27. e
28. g
29. h
30. e
31. a
32. f
33. c
34. d
35. b
36. b
37. a
38. g
39. e
40. d

41. f
42. c
43. a, c, d, e
44. b, d
45. a
46. b
47. a
48. a, c, e
49. d
50. We still carry the idea of one presiding authority, a judge, and peers who will help in the decision making process, a jury. A vassal would answer a summons.

1. F
2. T
3. F
4. F
5. T
6. T
7. T
8. F
9. T
10. T
11. a, b, c, e
12. c
13. h
14. g
15. b
16. i
17. f
18. e
19. d
20. a
21. c
22. e
23. c
24. d
25. h
26. f
27. g
28. l
29. b
30. k
31. i
32. j
33. a
34. a
35. b
36. b
37. conserve, liberate
38. facts
39. know, opinion
40. advertisers
41. audio, visual
42. "Face the Nation"
43. 1500s
44. neutrality
45. interfere or regulate religion
46. integration

47. 1963
48. freedom
49. Reagan
50. Judas
51. 5:9
52.
- Slavery will not prevent (or guarantee) salvation.
- Slavery not clearly forbidden; slaves instructed to be obedient and respectful, and to remain as slaves, although freedom is preferred("if you can gain your freedom, do so").
- Masters instructed to be compassionate
- Slave Traders equal to "the ungodly and sinful—the law is made not for the righteous but for lawbreakers and rebels

The Bible does not make a clear-cut case for or against slavery. Slavery was common in the culture of Bible times, but that doesn't make it right or wrong. Slavery was also common for nearly 250 years in North America, but it was eventually outlawed.

Scripture is clear that all people are to be treated with respect, for we are all made in God's image. Scripture is also clear that one's position in society, slave or free, rich or poor, will not prevent (or guarantee) salvation.

Slaves are instructed to be obedient and respectful, and to gain their freedom if possible; freedom is preferred. However, the runaway slave, Onesimus, is exhorted by Paul to return to his master. Masters are instructed to treat their slaves with compassion.

In 1 Timothy 1, slave traders are equated to "the ungodly and sinful." This may be due to greed, to mistreatment of slaves, or kidnapping, which was a common means of acquiring slaves. This verse is not clear evidence that slavery itself is evil.

Although some slaveholders in 19th century America used verses such as 1 Peter 2:18, Titus 2:9, and Colossians 3:22 to support the practice of slavery, they conveniently ignored verses such as Colossians 3:1 and 4:1.

1. j
2. k
3. m
4. i
5. l
6. g
7. f
8. h
9. e
10. d
11. a
12. c
13. b
14. j
15. k
16. i
17. h
18. f
19. d
20. e
21. g
22. c
23. b
24. a
25. higher
26. boon
27. resources
28. money
29. rise
30. railroads, mines
31. Africa
32. medium of exchange
33. gold
34. Adam Smith
35. raw materials
36. sales tactic
37. prosperity
38. gold
39. local banks, national currency, monetary
40. true
41. true
42. true
43. true
44. false
45. false
46. true
47. true
48. true
49. false
50. false
51. true
52. true
53. false
54. true
55. true
56. true
57. true
58. a, b, c, e, f
59. a, c, d
60. b
61. d
62. a, c, e
63. c, e
64. a

1. e
2. c
3. b
4. f
5. a
6. d
7. i
8. g
9. h
10. incentive
11. Clayton Antitrust Act
12. Board of Governors
13. credit, reserve
14. raise prices
15. Acting ethically
16. return policy, warranty
17. b
18. a
19. d
20. c
21. h
22. k
23. j
24. i
25. g
26. f
27. e
28. c
29. d
30. a
31. b
32. o
33. m
34. n
35. l
36. rebate
37. rob, Leviticus
38. entrepreneurship, operational management
39. communicate
40. masters, Master, fear
41. inflation
42. electric companies
43. stock market
44. purchasing, technological advances
45. bankruptcy court

46. continual debt
47. provide not for his own, infidel
48. stock market
49. checking account
50. borrows from
51. f
52. e
53. b
54. d
55. c
56. a
57. T
58. T
59. T
60. F
61. T
62. T
63. T
64. T
65. T
66.
    - Higher prices
    - No rival competition or alternative markets
    - Lower quality
    - Limitation or elimination of certain goods
    - Poor service and attitude
67.
    - open-market operations (purchase or sale of government securities)
    - change the discount rate
    - change reserve requirements
68.
    - If the car dealer will not or cannot show you the repair orders or identity of former owner, you should not buy the car.
    - Have a mechanic friend look for hidden damage repairs on "new" (and used) cars.
69.
    - top management
    - board of directors
70. debtors
71.
    - The Federal Communications Commission regulates radio and television to the extent of licensing stations and policing programming.

- The Federal Aviation Administration regulates the airlines.
- The Securities and Exchange Commission regulates the stock market.
- The Interstate Commerce Commission polices monopolistic practices.
- The Food and Drug Administration assesses all foods and drugs consumed.

72. liquidation

73. The 12 Federal Reserve Banks are nationwide, and each serves as a specific region of the country; along with the Board of Governors in Washington, D.C.

74. Either answer:

One of the largest divestitures in American history occurred when the U.S. Government ruled that the AT&T® Corporation was a monopoly that must be divided so that the telephone market might be more competitive.

Week by week the finances in this country can change, so the selling and buying of securities helps maintain equilibrium.

1. risk
2. net
3. little
4. margin, risk
5. earnings, year
6. Belgium
7. AMEX®
8. share
9. Industrial Revolution
10. share
11. not good enough
12. prospectus
13. purchasing
14. reports, house
15. commission
16. dividend
17. common, common, common
18. profit
19. product
20. grow
21. gambling
22. price, price
23. Crash
24. more harsh or worse
25. b
26. f
27. h
28. a
29. d
30. c
31. g
32. e
33. h
34. b
35. e
36. g
37. a
38. d
39. f
40. c
41. g
42. d

43. e
44. f
45. b
46. c
47. a
48. true
49. true
50. true
51. true
52. true
53. false
54.
   - The New York Stock Exchange® is also known by its initials, NYSE®.
   - Englands first stock exchange began in 1773.
   - The New York Stock Exchange® began with a handful of men standing in front of a buttonwood tree near the Trinity Church in East Manhattan during the American Revolution.
55. tickers
56.
   - The Standard & Poor® list contains the 500 largest publicly held companies.
   - First, all the common stock in a company must be issued. Then the company will begin to issue preferred stock.
   - Your portfolio is all of the various stocks or bonds you, as an investor, hold.
   - If the company has been making a good profit against competition, you may continue to see that profit grow and that is a good sign for investing.
   - Putting money into stocks is a risky thing.
57. mutual funds
58. Do not invest any money that you can't afford to lose.

1.	personal identification number	43.	true
2.	transfer funds	44.	true
3.	passbook	45.	true
4.	profit, service	46.	false
5.	charges	47.	true
6.	cooperative	48.	true
7.	traveler's checks	49.	c
8.	refund policy	50.	e
9.	60	51.	b
10.	increase, savings	52.	f
11.	minimum balance	53.	d
12.	bank balance	54.	a
13.	expenses, income	55.	b
14.	defer	56.	d
15.	Interest	57.	e
16.	credit bureaus	58.	b
17.	knowledge, power	59.	b
18.	credit limit	60.	b
19.	withhold	61.	a
20.	d	62.	b, c
21.	h	63.	a, b
22.	a		
23.	j		
24.	i		
25.	c		
26.	f		
27.	b		
28.	e		
29.	g		
30.	false		
31.	false		
32.	true		
33.	true		
34.	true		
35.	false		
36.	true		
37.	true		
38.	true		
39.	true		
40.	true		
41.	false		
42.	true		

1.	right	46.	f	
2.	25 (28)	47.	d	
3.	water	48.	a	
4.	Netherlands	49.	c	
5.	one quarter	50.	b	
6.	Victoria	51.	a	
7.	49,401	52.	c	
8.	Northeast	53.	b	
9.	Dover	54.	d	
10.	Norway	55.	f	
11.	Kyoto	56.	e	
12.	Norway	57.	F	
13.	privatizing	58.	T	
14.	tariffs	59.	F	
15.	second	60.	T	
16.	-84° *or* 84 degrees below zero	61.	T	
17.	Haifa	62.	T	
18.	Burma, Canada, Tunisia	63.	T	
19.	Acts chapter 11	64.	you don't get off the train	
20.	b	65.	Pakistan	
21.	f	66.	7	
22.	a		5	
23.	e		6	
24.	d		4	
25.	c		1	
26.	e		2	
27.	d		3	
28.	c			
29.	f			
30.	a			
31.	b			
32.	c			
33.	f			
34.	b			
35.	e			
36.	a			
37.	g			
38.	d			
39.	h			
40.	c			
41.	a			
42.	g			
43.	e			
44.	b			
45.	i			

1. F

2. F

3. F

4. T

5. F

6. T

7. F

8. F

9. two thirds

10. Prime Minister

11. the Senate, House of Representatives

12. House of Commons, House of Lords

13. dictatorships

14. *Das Kapital, The Communist Manifesto*

15. salvation

16. Daniel

17. Habeas Corpus

18. pluralist, or pluralistic

19. They enforce rules that control conduct within a population.

20. tangible, intangible

21. PRI (Institutional Revolutionary Party)

(any five of the following, any order):

22.–26.   France, Sri Lanka, Japan, Belgium, Italy, Denmark

27. e

28. a

29. c

30. f

31. b

32. d

33. 1 Timothy 2:1-4

34. communist

1. T
2. T
3. T
4. F
5. T
6. T
7. F
8. T
9. F
10. T

11. 10
12. draft
13. changes, amendments
14. House
15. interpret
16. diplomatic relations
17. nullify
18. divided government
19. Article I
20. 1787
21. ambassador
22. "domestic tranquility"
23. state government
24. redress
25. either: immunities, freedoms, or rights
26. Eighth
27. making laws and enforcing them
28. legislation
29. Second Amendment

30. d
31. c
32. a
33. b

34. Having agencies outside of Washington, D.C. helps fight the "Beltway mentality."

35. • National Security Council
    • Office of Policy Development

36. d
37. e
38. a
39. f
40. c
41. b

42. a
43. b
44. c

45. e
46. c
47. d
48. f
49. b
50. a

51. • The right to peaceably assemble is found in the First Amendment.
    • The first ten Amendments to the Constitution are called the Bill of Rights.
    • The Tenth Amendment gives states certain freedoms and control.

1. Canada, Great Britain, U.S.
2. (any 6): Jackson, Van Buren, Polk, Pierce, Buchanan, Cleveland, Wilson, Tyler, Roosevelt, Truman, Kennedy, Johnson, Carter, Clinton
3. electoral college
4. Conservative
5. Washington, D.C.
6. Breckinridge, Douglas
7. (any 5): Progressive Party, Bull Moose Party, Dixiecrats Party, American Independent Party, Liberal Republicans Party, Gold Democrats Party, Greenback Party, Socialist Party, Social Workers Party, Prohibition Party, American Communist Party, New Party, Natural Law Party, United We Stand Party, Reform Party, Libertarian Party, The Green Party, The US Taxpayers Party,

   Communist Party U.S.A.
8. a party that has only one goal
9. Federalists
10. strict construction
11. (private) donations
12. *The Republican*
13. single
14. 400
15. business
16. notary public, clerk
17. split ticket
18. unopposed
19. referendum
20. F
21. T
22. F
23. T
24. T
25. F
26. F

27. T
28. T
29. T
30. a. Stephen Douglas, d. John Breckinridge
31. a. United We Stand Party
32. b. The president could give asylum to any immigrant he wished.
33. d
34. e
35. b
36. f
37. a
38. c
39. a, b, c, e
40. d
41. c
42. a
43. b
44. b
45. d
46. a
47. e
48. c
49. a, b, c, d
50. b
51. the caucus assures absolute secrecy
52. b
53. c
54. a
55. e
56. d
57. a, b, c, e

1. true
2. false
3. false
4. true
5. true
6. true
7. false
8. false
9. false

10. [the] Concilum Plebus
11. Athens
12. 750 B.C.
13. patrician
14. subinfeudation
15. theocracy
16. Muhammed
17. death
18. the citizens freedom, opportunity for education, equality before the law, voting rights.
19. II
20. Gestapo
21. Great Depression

22. b
23. c
24. a
25. e
26. f
27. d
28. c
29. b

30. a
31. e
32. d
33. g
34. f
35. h
36. a
37. d
38. c
39. b
40. e
41. f

42. b, d, e, h, i

43. a
44. a

45. a
46. d

47. a, c

48. b

49. We still carry the idea of one presiding authority, a judge, and peers who will help in the decision making process, a jury. A vassal would answer a summons.

1. false
2. true
3. false
4. true
5. true
6. false
7. true
8. true
9. true
10. false
11. a, b, d
12. i
13. h
14. g
15. d
16. f
17. e
18. c
19. b
20. a
21. i
22. g
23. f
24. j
25. h
26. e
27. c
28. b
29. a
30. d
31. a, b, c, d, f, g
32. b
33. c
34. conserve, liberate
35. father, continent
36. particular problem
37. Gallup
38. Matthew 24:4
39. editors
40. "Meet the Press"
41. Parochial Schools

42. Romans 10:12
43. social rewards
44. love
45. plain folks
46. We are to put away strife and pride, and esteem others higher than ourselves.

1. h
2. j
3. i
4. f
5. e
6. g
7. d
8. c
9. a
10. b

11. h
12. g
13. f
14. e
15. d
16. c
17. b
18. i
19. a

20. wheat
21. lower
22. money
23. wage-price spiral
24. work
25. CIO, AFL
26. medium of exchange
27. Adam Smith
28. exploration
29. sales tactic
30. yen
31. Greenback
32. 1800s
33. regulating, local banks, national currency

34. true
35. false
36. true
37. false
38. true
39. true
40. true
41. true
42. true
43. false
44. true
45. false
46. true
47. false
48. false
49. true
50. false

51. a, b, d
52. b, c, d

53. e

54. b, c, d, f, g, h, j
55. a, c, e
56. b

1. f
2. g
3. d
4. e
5. c
6. a
7. b

8. purchasing power
9. Clayton Antitrust Act
10. divestitures
11. raise prices

12. a
13. b
14. c
15. d

16. securities
17. credit, reserve
18. independent
19. Internet

20. h
21. i
22. g
23. e
24. f
25. a
26. c
27. d
28. b
29. k
30. j

31. By hanging on to a car for ten years instead of making a new purchase with a trade-in every three years or so, a car owner can save $400,00–$450,000 over a period of 40 years, even considering the higher costs for the repair of the older car.

32. inventory
33. rob, Leviticus
34. profit or loss
35. go between or broker
36. fairness
37. safety
38. stock market
39. purchasing, technological advances
40. 4

41. b
42. c
43. e
44. d
45. a

46. continual debt
47. provide not for his own, infidel
48. stock market
49. one-third

50. b
51. a

52. T
53. T
54. F
55. T
56. T
57. T
58. F

59.
- Higher prices
- No rival competition or alternative markets
- Lower quality
- Limitation or elimination of certain goods
- Poor service and attitude

60.
- The U.S. Treasury, through its Bureau of the Mint and Bureau of Engraving and Printing, produces the nation's dollar and coin supply.
- The Fed issues the nation's coin and paper currency.
- Trusts were unofficial mergers formed to control prices and production in the marketplace.
- Some monopolies are good.
- The Interstate Commerce Commission polices monopolistic practices.

61.
- After passage of the 1996 deregulation law the Baby Bells started merging with each other, and two of them attempted to re-merge into AT&T®.
- A lone utility company, Detroit Edison and Consumers Power, faced new competition as deregulation gave people a choice between utility companies.
- Those that are in support of something are called its proponents.

62. The business actually added less to the box–and kept the price the same.

63. the day to day operation of a business

64. At the local level, businesses must meet government-set billing rates.

65.
- The Federal Communications Commission regulates radio and television to the extent of licensing stations and policing programming.
- The Federal Aviation Administration regulates the airlines.
- The Securities and Exchange Commission regulates the stock market.
- The Interstate Commerce Commission polices monopolistic practices.
- The Food and Drug Administration assesses all foods and drugs consumed.

66. Deregulated Investor Owned Utilities are known as IOUs.

67.
- In a Chapter 13 proceeding, the debtor surrenders their nonexempt property for division among their creditors.
- Monopolies are judged by how strong the competition is between the companies.

68. The 12 Federal Reserve Banks are nationwide, and each serves a specific region of the country; along with the Board of Governors in Washington, D.C.

1. Depression
2. little
3. actual number
4. earnings, year
5. floor
6. Belgium
7. Industrial Revolution
8. cash
9. prospectus
10. services or commission
11. purchasing
12. employee
13. AT&T®, Boeing®
14. dividend
15. Blue chip stocks
16. profit
17. retail
18. competition
19. stockholder
20. skeptical
21. gambling
22. 89
23. more harsh or worse
24. c
25. d
26. h
27. b
28. g
29. a
30. f
31. e
32. h
33. d
34. f
35. g
36. e
37. a
38. b
39. c
40. e
41. d
42. c

43. f
44. b
45. a
46. true
47. false
48. true
49. true
50. true
51. true
52. transaction
53.
   - The Wall Street Journal® is the daily newspaper which focuses on stock market activity.
   - People will subscribe to publications such as Barron's® or The Wall Street Journal® to get information on investing more wisely.
   - Mattel®, as well as thousands of other companies, offers the opportunity to buy a part of their company by selling shares.
54. tickers
55.
   - The Standard & Poor® list contains the 500 largest publicly held companies.
   - First, all the common stock in a company must be issued. Then the company will begin to issue preferred stock.
   - Your portfolio is all of the various stocks or bonds you, as an investor, hold.
   - If the company has been making a good profit against competition, you may continue to see that profit grow and that is a good sign for investing.
   - Putting money into stocks is a risky thing.
56. When the market is trying to steady itself out after a monumental movement, it is called a correction.

1.	personal identification number	36.	false
2.	Processing a loan	37.	true
3.	profit, service	38.	true
4.	installment, home	39.	true
5.	Travelers checks	40.	true
6.	issuing	41.	true
7.	Visa	42.	false
8.	paychecks	43.	true
9.	increase, savings	44.	false
10.	rich	45.	d
11.	expenses, income	46.	e
12.	deferment	47.	b
13.	Interest	48.	a
14.	credit bureaus	49.	c
15.	credit limit		
16.	affinity	50.	b
		51.	d
17.	j	52.	b
18.	i		
19.	h	53.	c
20.	g	54.	a
21.	e	55.	e
22.	f	56.	b
23.	d		
24.	c	57.	b
25.	b	58.	c, d
26.	a	59.	b, c
		60.	a, b, d
27.	true	61.	a, b
28.	false		
29.	true		
30.	false		
31.	true		
32.	true		
33.	true		
34.	true		
35.	true		

1.	France	37.	f
2.	European	38.	i
3.	Netherlands	39.	c
4.	Portugal	40.	a
5.	Frankfurt	41.	h
6.	Germany	42.	e
7.	Protestants	43.	g
8.	dependent areas	44.	b
9.	Oklahoma	45.	c
10.	fjords	46.	a
11.	70	47.	b
12.	sun	48.	a
13.	an Israeli	49.	c
14.	zayat	50.	c
15.	martyr	51.	a
16.	Pacific Ocean, along the US border, Gulf of Mexico	52.	b
17.	Belize	53.	T
18.	c	54.	F
19.	a	55.	T
20.	f	56.	F
21.	b	57.	F
22.	e	58.	F
23.	d	59.	F
24.	h	60.	British Columbia
25.	g	61.	Oregon, Salem
26.	h		Maine, Augusta
27.	g		Michigan, Lansing
28.	f		Louisiana, Baton Rouge
29.	a		North Carolina, Raleigh
30.	e		Montana, Helena
31.	b		
32.	d		
33.	c		
34.	j		
35.	d		
36.	b		